RETHINKING
SOCIAL MEDIA
AND EXTREMISM

RETHINKING SOCIAL MEDIA AND EXTREMISM

EDITED BY SHIRLEY LEITCH AND PAUL PICKERING

Australian
National
University

ANU PRESS

AUSTRALIA AND THE WORLD

ANU PRESS

Published by ANU Press
The Australian National University
Canberra ACT 2600, Australia
Email: anupress@anu.edu.au

Available to download for free at press.anu.edu.au

ISBN (print): 9781760465247
ISBN (online): 9781760465254

WorldCat (print): 1317737911
WorldCat (online): 1317738078

DOI: 10.22459/RSME.2022

Cover design and layout by ANU Press

This book is published under the aegis of the Australia and the World Editorial Board of ANU Press.

Contents

Foreword

Sophisticated democracies feel increasingly as if at war with themselves, vacating the centre ground and succumbing to a divisive politics. Regrettably, the last few years in Britain and the US exemplify this point.

Facilitated by the swift and universal access to social media, heated disagreement is endemic in public discourse.

The scholars brought together for this thoughtful collection of essays were motivated by the egregious inhumanity of the deadly Christchurch mosque attacks of 2019, and the failures of governance, security and community that contributed to it.

But the attention of these authors is far wider.

From an array of perspectives, they consider the wellsprings of religious and politically motivated violent extremism, the exponential growth and contributory role of social media platforms, the extent and influence of hyper-violent gaming, the shortcomings of internet regulation, and the ways in which these developments both reflect history and threaten to overturn it.

Their conclusions are challenging in multiple ways, inviting readers to look beyond glib solutions like blunt censorship, deplatforming and heavy-handed government restrictions of free speech.

Yet they also ask us to consider the ways in which an overall atmosphere of incivility has become normalised, suggesting that the absence of social standards in cyberspace may validate and even concentrate grievance and intolerance.

For some (usually anonymous) individuals, this disinhibits the public expression of misogyny, homophobia and racism – forms of hate speech that, while not always causal, invariably precede violent extremism when it does occur.

This book is the first in a bold series from The Australian National University's Australian Studies Institute and I'm delighted to commend it to readers interested in this and the rich variety of subject offerings to come.

I would also like to personally congratulate the editors of this timely volume, professors Shirley Leitch and Paul Pickering for their outstanding work in compiling it.

Professor Brian P. Schmidt AC FAA FRS
Vice-Chancellor
The Australian National University

Acknowledgements

We would like to thank all those who participated in the 'After Christchurch: Violent Extremism Online' workshop in August 2019, including those who have not contributed a chapter to this volume: Lesley Seebeck, Alison Dundes Renteln, Xinyuan (Cynthia) Xu and Seth Lazar. Their papers and their contributions to the discussion enriched it and thereby helped to provide impetus to the idea of putting together a volume of essays devoted to the broader theme of social media and extremism.

The readers who peer reviewed the collection provided many helpful insights, comments and suggestions that undeniably improved it. Your generous contributions are recognised and appreciated.

We also would like to acknowledge our proofreader, Barbara Coe, for her meticulous attention to the manuscript. Our thanks too to Roxanne Missingham, ANU Librarian and Director of ANU Press, for her support and encouragement. As an open-access university press, ANU Press plays a central and crucial role in sharing Australian scholarship with the world, and were the natural choice of publisher.

Many thanks, as always, to the Australian Studies Institute's professional staff. Fiona Preston has managed this project from the first word to the last, wrangling authors and editors alike. Jemima Parker also contributed all along the way, including designing the riveting cover.

Finally, and to paraphrase an old joke, we also acknowledge the pandemic, without which this book would have been finished sooner.

Abbreviations

ACCC	Australian Competition and Consumer Commission
AFP	Australian Federal Police
AI	artificial intelligence
ATCTEVMO	Australian Taskforce to Combat Terrorist and Extreme Violent Material Online
AVC	abhorrent violent conduct
AVM	abhorrent violent material
BBC	British Broadcasting Corporation
BCE	before the Common Era
CEO	Chief Executive Officer
CNN	Cable News Network
CSR	corporate social responsibility
Cth	Commonwealth
DC	District of Columbia
DDOS	distributed denial of service
EU	European Union
FBI	Federal Bureau of Investigation
FTC	Federal Trade Commission
G20	Group of Twenty
G7	Group of Seven
GIFCT	Global Internet Forum to Counter Terrorism
HTTP	HyperText Transfer Protocol
incel	involuntary celibate
ISIS	Islamic State of Iraq and Syria

ISP	Internet Service Provider
IT	information technology
MFAT	Ministry of Foreign Affairs and Trade (Aotearoa New Zealand)
MGAFA	Microsoft, Google, Apple, Facebook and Amazon
MP	Member of Parliament
NCA	National Capital Authority (Australia)
NGO	non-government organisation
OSPs	online service providers
PJCIS	Parliamentary Joint Committee on Intelligence and Security
PM	Prime Minister
PvE	person versus environment games
PvP	person versus person games
SNS	social networking sites
STEM	science, technology, engineering and mathematics
UK	United Kingdom
UN	United Nations
UNHRC	United Nations Human Rights Council
US	United States
USDoJ	United States Department of Justice
VEO	violent extremism online

Contributors

Dominique Dalla-Pozza is a senior lecturer at the Law School, ANU College of Law, working in the field of Australian Public Law and Australian National Security Law. Her primary research deals with the Australian Parliament and the legislative process, especially the process by which Australian National Security Law is made. She is particularly interested in the work done by parliamentary committees. Her PhD (completed at the Gilbert+Tobin Centre of Public Law at UNSW) focused on the process by which the Australian Parliament enacted counterterrorism legislation between 2001 and 2006.

Robert Fleet is a PhD candidate at the Centre for Digital Humanities Research, ANU. His primary research interests look at patterns of behaviour in virtual worlds and what they tell us about patterns observed in the physical world as they apply to organised criminal groups. Robert was previously an e-research analyst and works as a consultant data scientist at the University of Canberra.

Katrina Grant is a senior lecturer at the Centre for Digital Humanities Research, ANU. She is an art historian and digital humanities researcher with a background in the study of Early Modern Italy. Her research focuses on gardens and the history of landscapes, the visual culture of theatre and festivals, and the application of digital methods to research on visual cultures.

Andrew Hughes is a lecturer in marketing in the Research School of Management, ANU. He teaches marketing at both undergraduate and postgraduate levels and is considered to be one of the leading researchers in political marketing in Australia. He has given numerous interviews on politics and political marketing to international and national television, print and internet outlets.

Mark Kenny is a professor at the Australian Studies Institute, ANU. He came to ANU after a high-profile journalistic career as chief political correspondent and national affairs editor of the *Sydney Morning Herald* and the *Age*. Host of the ANU podcast 'Democracy Sausage', Mark is a widely reported commentator on politics, both in Australia and internationally. His research interests include democracy, legitimacy and populism.

Shirley Leitch is an emerita professor and professorial fellow at the Australian Studies Institute, ANU. She joined the institute after serving ANU first as dean of the College of Business and Economics and then as deputy vice-chancellor (global engagement). Her research is focused on public discourse and change, including science–society engagement in relation to controversial science and technology. Shirley is also the founding chair of successful education technology company, Online Education Services Ltd.

Mark Nolan is Director of the Centre for Law and Justice at Charles Sturt University and an honorary professor (adjunct) at the ANU College of Law. He is an interdisciplinary legal scholar with qualifications in law, honours and doctoral training in social psychology, and a Masters of Asia Pacific Studies majoring in Thai language. Prior to becoming director at CSU, Mark worked at the ANU College of Law where he taught undergraduate and postgraduate students and researched criminal law and procedure.

Terhi Nurmikko-Fuller is a senior lecturer in digital humanities at the Centre for Digital Humanities Research, ANU. She focuses on interdisciplinary experimentation into the ways digital technologies can support and diversify research in the humanities, arts and social sciences, and in relation to public culture (including web science and the galleries, libraries, archives and museums sector). Her research covers linked data projects for humanities data, 3D modelling and how the online world affects education and learning.

Paul Pickering is Director of the Australian Studies Institute (2017–), ANU. Paul has undertaken numerous roles at ANU, including as dean of the College of Arts and Social Sciences (2014–16), director of the Research School of Humanities and the Arts (2013–21), inaugural director of the ANU Centre for European Studies (2010–12), director of Graduate Studies (2004–09) and a Queen Elizabeth II Fellow at the

Humanities Research Centre (2000–04). He is a fellow of the Royal Historical Society. In 2012 he was the recipient of the Vice-Chancellor's Award for Excellence in Graduate Supervision.

Sally Wheeler OBE MRIA FAcSS FAAL is Deputy Vice-Chancellor (International Strategy) and Dean of Law at ANU. Prior to taking up these positions, Sally was a professor and pro vice-chancellor for Research and Enterprise at Queen's University, Belfast. She was elected to the Academy of Social Sciences and the Royal Irish Academy in 2011 and 2013, respectively. She became a fellow of the Australian Academy of Law in 2018.

1

Rethinking social media and extremism

Shirley Leitch and Paul Pickering

Terrorism has entered the mainstream of twenty-first century life, with seemingly random attacks in civilian spaces a tragic staple of the daily news flow. Even a global pandemic has not slowed the pace, with the United Nations (2021) warning that terrorists are exploiting our growing, COVID-driven dependence on cyberspace. The innovative use of digital technology for the purposes of terror was a central feature of the 2019 Christchurch massacre and the attack put a spotlight on the prominent role of social media in propagating violent extremism. Christchurch was noteworthy for many other reasons, not least that the neo-fascist affiliation of the gunman clashed with the dominant fear of Islamist terrorism. However, it was the central role of social media that stood out. Put starkly: Facebook livestreamed this massacre. While the terrorist was cast as a 'lone gunman', he was anything but alone. Through cyberspace, he had connected with a global network of neo-fascists dedicated to upholding white supremacy in the West. Social media was implicated in every aspect of the Christchurch terror attack – in its inspiration, planning, preparation, execution and ongoing mythic status. It is the relationship between social media and extremism that binds the multiple perspectives within this book together.[1] The book offers reflections from a range of

---

1   The chapters within this book were first workshopped at the symposium 'After Christchurch: Violent Extremism Online', hosted by the Australian Studies Institute at The Australian National University, 29 August 2019.

disciplinary perspectives but it is in no way intended to be comprehensive either in scope or subject. Rather we see it as an intervention, a provocation and an attempt to bring a multidisciplinary lens to a wicked problem for which there are no risk-free solutions.

Online environments – most commonly social media – are now as important as real-world spaces in shaping and enabling acts of terrorism, amplifying their impact and constraining the ability of nation-states to prevent future attacks. The causes, contributing factors and effects of terrorism are so complex that terrorism itself may be seen as a 'wicked problem' that resists simple solutions. It is necessary to invite many perspectives and areas of expertise to the table if we are to address such crises. Any analysis of the genesis of a crisis event like the Christchurch massacre – as well as any attempt to understand how we might reduce the risk of such events in future – leads us rapidly down many interconnected paths. Freedom of speech, globalisation, the adequacy of legal and regulatory frameworks, corporate self-governance, monopoly capitalism, national sovereignty, the rise of populism, the decline of civility, online extremism, fake news and misinformation, and the myriad connections between these issues and the nature of terrorism itself all surface in the following chapters.

Throughout the book, a recurring theme is the role of former US president Donald Trump in enabling the rise of right-wing extremism. During the Trump presidency, neo-fascist groups emerged from the shadows into the mainstream of political discourse. The administration was openly linked with the so-called 'alt-right', anti-Islamist and anti-immigration rhetoric of Breitbart News and other far-right websites, with President Trump even declaring that there were 'very fine people on both sides' following the murder of a woman protesting against a neo-fascist rally in Charlottesville, Virginia (Reilly, 2017). His statements went far beyond dog-whistling, reaching an apotheosis on 6 January 2021 when he urged a crowd assembled to march on Congress to 'fight like hell' to save their country and later gave succour to the violent mob in the process of ransacking the Capitol Building that he loved them and that they were very special. At the same time as Trump's words were being broadcast to the nation, the insurrection itself was also being livestreamed via mainstream social media platforms as well as on a plethora of sites living in what Rebecca Heilweil and Shirin Ghaffary (2021) have called the 'dark corners of the internet'. The complicity of Trump and his acolytes in the events of 6 January grabbed the headlines and the insurrection also shone a spotlight of the awesome and unfettered power of social media.

At the time of the Christchurch massacre it was already clear that US-based social media giants, such as Facebook and Alphabet, were providing global, digital platforms for terrorism. After Christchurch, these companies faced multiple threats from US conservatives, not because of their role in enabling extremist networks to flourish but because they took action against some far-right sites and contributors. In the face of such threats – especially of antitrust suits – social media companies have been constrained in their ability and, arguably, their motivation to eliminate content linked to alt-right terrorism. Meanwhile, global censure of, and pressure on, these companies continued to grow.

While international condemnation of the Christchurch massacre was swift, that has been the case following every terrorist attack. Leitch argues in the following chapter that attempts to take action are continually hampered by the competing political agendas, economic drivers and technological capabilities of the actors involved. In the immediate aftermath of the attack, when images of the victims – including small children and elderly men – were still circulating in the media, world leaders came together in Paris to sign up to the Christchurch Call to Action to combat violent extremism online. The US, however, remained an outlier, refusing to sign up to the call and citing free speech concerns about the agreement. In a move that directly undermined the call, the Trump presidency launched its own attack in the opposite direction, including an online tool to report any suspected censorship of conservative opinions directly to the White House. In a tweet supportive of his father's stance, Donald Trump Junior accused the so-called 'Big Tech monopoly men' of the 'purposeful and calculated silencing of conservatives' (Trump Jr, 2019). Given that the major nations were so divided over the problem to be solved, it should be no surprise that the numerous agreements signed and voluntary commitments made have not put an end to violent extremism online or that real-world attacks have continued.

The gravity of the events of 6 January in the heart of US democracy was, however, seen by many commentators as not only producing a hitherto elusive consensus among lawmakers about the need to act but also as a turning point for the barons of social media platforms. As noted, it was clear that the major platforms had failed to moderate outrageous content on their platforms and allowed the attack on the Capitol to be organised, coordinated and celebrated right under their noses. As Nurmikko-Fuller and Pickering discuss in their chapter, attempts at self-regulation by Facebook have been widely criticised and, as recent whistleblowers attest, enthusiasm for self-regulation is waning in the sector. The political consensus quickly evaporated during Trump's impeachment trials. Although online posts are now being used widely in the prosecution of the rioters, there is little else to cheer about. Moreover, as Leitch observes, it is ironic that the monopoly status and profits that social media companies seek to protect within the US will ensure that extremist content will continue to be globally distributed, increasing the chance that national and supranational regulation will be introduced.

One of the primary stumbling blocks for nations taking action in relation to online extremism is the relatively recent genesis of the internet and the novelty of the innovations it has afforded. The near instantaneous and global connectivity enabled by digital technology has created whole new industries along with mega corporations. Seven of the world's top 10 companies are now technology companies, including Facebook, Alphabet, Tencent, Alibaba and Amazon. The national and international rules governing such behemoths were written, for the most part, prior to the advent of the internet. Legislative frameworks designed for the analogue age have proven wholly inadequate to the task of tackling a raft of new and serious issues, including violent extremism, online. While policymakers struggle through a growing backlog of legislation, corporations have been largely left to their own devices, self-regulating in ways that best support their business models. The technology companies themselves have expanded so rapidly from homegrown startups to trillion-dollar corporations that their own internal governance has been frequently found wanting. The urgency of transforming these adolescent companies into adult, civic actors is considered in Chapter 3.

Much has already been written about the wisdom of the legal exemptions enjoyed by technology companies with internet platforms that protect them from liability for the content posted by their users. These legal protections are critical to the continuing expansion of social media companies. As Seth Oranburg (2021) has noted:

> Twitter, Facebook, Instagram, YouTube, TikTok, Reddit and Discord are not subject to First Amendment constraints because they are not state actors. These platforms do not 'censor' speech, in the technical sense, because only governments can censor. Private actors merely exercise editorial discretion – and they may do so virtually at will.

What this means is that in the US social media platforms are not liable for defamatory or inflammatory tweets.

In the absence of liability for the harm that their content may cause, companies are able to take a reactive stance that is reliant on algorithms and complaint-based responses, which pose minimal interruption to real-time postings. In Chapter 3, Wheeler not only maps out the problems but also moves us beyond them to consider deeper questions of corporate social responsibility, ethics and the social licence of businesses to operate. From this perspective, asking whether or not corporate activities are legal sets a very low bar for their behaviour. Rather than asking what they must do to avoid prosecution, we might ask what they *should* do to avoid damaging individuals and societies. Wheeler also contends that major companies that provide essential public services might be deemed public utilities and, for this reason alone, be subject to different rules and expectations from those of other types of businesses. The centrality of social media platforms to many critical services was demonstrated by Facebook itself when it blocked many sites during a disagreement with the Australian Government in 2021. The move provoked public discussion of the increasing reliance of government agencies, including emergency services, on a privately owned platform with no legal requirement to maintain those services.

While the dangers of unfettered, monopoly capitalism in the digital age are apparent, there are less obvious problems related to what Wheeler refers to as the 'tech stack'. There are layers of smaller players within the tech stack, comprising companies that are invisible to internet users, but provide the critical, technical services underpinning the platforms that are household names. In the largely self-regulating world of the internet, each of these players will have its own set of rules relating to, for example, the takedown of extremist content or denial of services to users who offend against these rules. Some companies have also proven resistant to enforcing any rules at all, arguing that it is beyond their remit to regulate free speech or to make decisions about what is and what is not acceptable content. Such was the case after the Christchurch massacre when companies – most notably Cloudflare – who had provided services to the 8chan website used by the terrorist, only took action after concerted public pressure.

It may seem obvious that terrorists should be denied access to services that assist them to commit atrocities. Equally, it may be simply self-serving of companies to eschew any responsibility for the actions of their terrorist clients in the name of free speech. Yet placing responsibility for controlling content and access wholly onto internet companies is by no means without its own dangers. Nor are the arguments made by the companies themselves that they are ill-equipped and unsuited to setting the rules entirely ill-founded. Wheeler advises caution when it comes to deplatforming users who profess extreme views. In the current era, the push for deplatforming has primarily emanated from the left and has been targeted at hate speech emanating from the extreme right. Yet, during the Cold War, it was the left who were targeted in what became known as the McCarthy era. Unfounded accusations destroyed the lives and careers of many people and created a climate of fear. The dangers of overreach and the difficulty of setting the rules of acceptable speech are evident, especially in the heat of the moment following a disturbing event involving multiple civilian deaths. Deplatforming extremist groups of any persuasion may also lend credence to their claims of victimisation and enhance their status with potential recruits. Wheeler warns that extremists may be pushed onto the dark web and into encrypted apps where their activities become less visible and harder to monitor.

There is already evidence that as Facebook and Twitter have increasingly blocked extremists, such users have simply moved to other online spaces. The chat platforms associated with video games, such as Twitch, have been a popular choice, especially in association with violent games that attract a mostly young and male following. Criticism of violent video games on the basis that the fantasy world of gaming may spill over into real-world violence has been common since their invention. For example, the 1999 Columbine High School massacre was linked with first-person shooter games *Doom* and *Quake*, which were played by the students who committed the massacre. An unsuccessful lawsuit against the manufacturers of these and similar games was even launched by the family of the slain teacher. The same arguments were made in connection with the Christchurch terrorist, who was widely reported in the media as having an 'addiction' to video gaming. The video game industry was therefore blamed alongside social media platforms for creating the violent mindset of the terrorist as well as supporting his actions. After all, one of the most disturbing aspects of the Christchurch massacre livestream was its framing as a first-person shooter video game and its subsequent re-emergence as an actual game. Rejecting the kneejerk reaction that Christchurch demonstrates a straightforward, causal connection between violent game content and real-world violent acts, Fleet suggests in Chapter 4 that it may actually be the reverse. It is our real-world knowledge, skills and predispositions – violent or otherwise – that we carry with us into the virtual world and enact through role-playing. Games may be more interesting for what they reveal about us than for what they cause us to do.

Over 90 per cent of teenagers in the developed world play video games and 90 per cent of the games involve violence of some kind. A major study conducted by Andrew Przybylski and Netta Weinstein (2019), published by the prestigious Royal Society in London, concluded that there was no evidence of a direct correlation between game play and subsequent mass-shooting events or violent behaviour more generally. Of course, their findings fly in the face of a widespread truism. Indeed, their conclusions highlight the fact that policymakers and governments are acting on the basis of a 'precautionary principle' rather than empirical research. In one sense, the debate is redundant: if over 90 per cent of young people play games and 90 per cent of the games they play involve violence then *ipso facto* only a tiny percentage of gamers end up as mass murders. Nevertheless, that miniscule percentage of potentially murderous gamers are prime candidates to be drawn into the dark parts of the web. Fleet notes that those who participate in underground games and associated chat groups also constitute the primary demographic of potential recruits for alt-right terrorist groups. Fleet describes the discourses surrounding these underground games as replete with neo-fascist, Identitarian, anti-immigration, racist, homophobic and misogynist themes. He contends that the neo-fascist ideology expressed by the Christchurch terrorist in his manifesto was well aligned with the casual conversation of this community. While community members rarely go on to commit terrorist attacks, they nonetheless provide the supportive environment that nurtures and then mythologises those who do.

Through gaming and social media, the internet has enabled extremists to establish and maintain close connections even in the absence of formal organisational structures and sometimes in the absence of any formal group at all. The commitment of these potential terrorists is ideological rather than organisational. In Chapter 5, Hughes argues that, from a marketing perspective, such ideologically based networks operate like brand communities with racism and misogyny as core brand values. In the alternative reality of extremist brand communities, terrorist attacks are legitimated as the virtuous actions of heroes who often sacrifice their lives for the cause. Their atrocities are celebrated and ranked by 'kill count'. Hughes explores the creation of intense emotional responses in individuals through social media as a possible antecedent to so-called 'lone wolf' attacks. While the gunmen may act alone, they are in fact acting out their attacks for their online brand community and in the name of shared values.

One of the primary responses to terrorism on the part of governments has been to ban extremist groups. This strategy has proven ineffective in combating the loosely coupled but emotionally intense networks of contemporary extremists. Instead, policy and regulatory responses now often seek to make technology companies more responsible for policing internet content. For example, the Australian Government's response to the Christchurch massacre was very much focused on internet service providers. Within weeks of the massacre, the *Criminal Code Amendment (Sharing of Abhorrent Violent Materials) Act 2019* (Cth) was rushed through both houses of the Australian Parliament and signed into law. Reportedly drafted in just 48 hours, the new law was always going to be subject to criticism, including for its potential violation of international law. The contentious elements of the law itself, the parliamentary debates that accompanied its passage and the questions raised in the Senate Estimates hearings in April 2019 are the focus of the chapter by Nolan and Dalla-Pozza. Their analysis teases out which elements of violent extremism online were given prominence by lawmakers and which were neglected. In doing so, they reveal how the problem was understood in the immediate aftermath of the massacre. They also identify important areas for future law reform.

There is no doubt that further – albeit more carefully worked through – law reform is needed. The opening up of virtual public space for alt-right hate speech has generated a plethora of new risks for societies. Continuing the theme of the rapid erosion of democratic and social norms in the digital age, Kenny identifies hateful discourses as longstanding levers of power in Australia and beyond. The era of digital self-publishing through social media has given prominence as well as fuel to existing dysfunctions within political discourse. The rise of supra internet companies has seen a corresponding fall in the ability of nation-states to regulate the public exchange of ideas or protect citizens from extremist content. Within democratic states and in a post-9/11 world, attempts to place limits on such content are waved through when they address external 'Islamist' threats, but are hotly contested in the name of 'free speech' when focused on internal, alt-right hate groups. Situating the tragedy within its broader cultural context, in his chapter, Kenny argues that the general decline of civility in public discourse has desensitised us to abhorrent views. Violent outbursts aimed at women, or immigrants, or minorities, or, indeed, at anyone who is perceived to be at odds with the speaker's identity or worldview, are normalised as though they had no real-world consequences. The step from mainstream public discourse to the hate speech of the dark web has narrowed and the latter has bled through into political life.

The effective regulation of cyberspace to reduce the risk of terrorism requires that we first recognise it as a space where actions carrying real-world consequences may be enacted. Events such as the Christchurch massacre have severely dented the net utopia of early internet advocates with their anarchic vision of a global space beyond the reach and comprehension of governments. In her chapter, Grant turns our attention to these spatial elements of the internet, both as a place for publicly debating democratic ideals, and for the performance of power by elites and reinforcement of social hierarchies. She invites us to compare social media platforms like Facebook and Twitter with the public squares and speakers' corners of the past. Both have enabled the dissemination of ideas – including the 'dangerous' ideas of revolution – and provided space for acts of rebellion and repression. Both have supported revelations and propaganda, and served the state and its enemies. Drawing on historical examples to find points of continuity and rupture, Grant illustrates how space has been negotiated differently in different epochs and cultures.

If we take the long view suggested by Grant, we find that each new communication technology has triggered concern, even panic, especially on the part of the powerful. It is fitting, then, to conclude this book by considering what is old and what is new about the digital age. Nurmikko-Fuller, the digital humanities scholar, debates this question with Pickering, the historian. The long view takes us back to 3400 BCE when an unknown accountant invented writing on clay tablets to keep track of the finances of the Temple of Inanna. So long as writing remained the preserve of the elite, Pickering contends, societies were largely content with communications for many thousands of years. However, the invention of the printing press started to broaden the production and distribution base of communication. Gutenberg's innovation of moveable type in the sixteenth century vastly increased the speed and flexibility of the printing process, while the electromechanical machines of the nineteenth century brought the written word within reach of all literate people. It was the printing press that sparked the first tech-panic among political elites who viewed the written word as a dangerous weapon in the hands of ordinary people. Democratisation of communication, they feared, would ignite revolution in Europe. Pickering suggests that the same kinds of anti-democratic arguments for limiting the use of the printing press to spread 'socially constructed extremist ideas' are being used currently to support the heavy-handed regulation and state control of the internet. Viewed in this way, the internet appears less a profound break with the past than a new site of an age-old contest for power.

In her counterpoint, Nurmikko-Fuller sets out an equally compelling case that the internet has changed everything. While agreeing that elite fear of popular communication is an historical constant, Nurmikko-Fuller argues that the internet age is best understood as a point of rupture. The printing press is a one-to-many communication tool, as are broadcast media. Instantaneous, interactive and with an in-built panoptic surveillance function, the internet is fundamentally different. The growth of social media has seen individuals unknowingly, as well as voluntarily, surrendering data and privacy to corporations and governments. Vast databases of aggregated personal information are then used to manipulate everything from mundane purchase decisions to the choices we make at the ballot box. At the same time, we have opened our lives to a whole new set of criminal actors. The scene is set for political corruption, cybercrime and the ongoing erosion of the private sphere. Seen from this perspective, the internet is far more than just the latest in a long line of communication technologies. Where Pickering and Nurmikko-Fuller come together is in relation to concerns over the increasing concentration of ownership and control over the internet in the hands of a small number of poorly regulated companies, along with the privatisation of the personal data that their platforms collect.

Our goal in this book is to offer a series of broad-ranging reflections on violent extremism online and how to stop it. It was the sheer horror and magnitude of the Christchurch massacre that brought such a diverse group of scholars together. If there is a shared conclusion, it is the realisation of just how ill-equipped we are – nationally here in Australia and internationally – to deal with the globally connected world of the internet. Our legal and regulatory frameworks were designed for an analogue age and have not proven fit for purpose in the face of multiple new perils including cybercrime, electoral fraud and the 'fake news' that has fuelled the rise of populism. Government responses have proven to be wholly inadequate. Policymakers struggle to understand the magnitude of the changes that the internet has wrought or to keep pace with the speed of its development. And, what of our rights as citizens? As politicians and lawyers run to catch up to the future as it disappears over the horizon, who guarantees our right to free speech, to free and fair elections, to play video games, to surf the net, to believe 'fake news'? As one major crisis follows another and a global pandemic accelerates our turn to digital technologies, attending to the issues raised in this book becomes ever more urgent. Clearly, there is much to discuss and more books to write.

References

Heilweil, R. & Ghaffary, S. (2021). How Trump's internet built and broadcast the Capitol insurrection. *Vox*. Retrieved from www.vox.com/recode/22221285/trump-online-capitol-riot-far-right-parler-twitter-facebook.

Oranburg, S. C. (2021). Social media and democracy after the Capitol riot. *Duquesne Lawyer*. Retrieved from www.duq.edu/academics/schools/law/alumni/duquesne-lawyer-magazine/social-media-and-democracy-after-the-capitol-riot.

Przybylski, A. K. & Weinstein, N. (2019). Violent video game engagement is not associated with adolescents' aggressive behaviour: Evidence from a registered report. *Royal Society Open Science*. doi.org/10.1098/rsos.171474.

Reilly, K. (2017, 15 August). President Trump again blames 'both sides' for Charlottesville violence. *Time*. Retrieved from time.com/4902129/president-donald-trump-both-sides-charlottesville/.

Trump, Donald Jr. (2019, 4 May). @DonaldJTrumpJr, 1.46 am. Twitter.com.

UN (United Nations). (2021). *Remarks at the Second High-Level Conference of Heads of Counter-Terrorism Agencies of Member States*, by António Guterres. Retrieved from www.un.org/sg/en/content/sg/speeches/2021-06-28/remarks-second-high-level-conference-of-heads-of-counter-terrorism-agencies-of-member-states.

2

The making of a 'made for social media' massacre

Shirley Leitch

On 15 March 2019, Facebook livestreamed a massacre. A lone gunman toting semi-automatic weapons killed 51 people and wounded 49 others.[1] Two mosques in the small city of Christchurch were the physical location of the attack but this massacre was planned and executed for a much larger audience. As a prelude, the terrorist posted a 'Great Replacement' manifesto online and emailed a personal copy to the prime minister of New Zealand. Comprising 87 pages of racist memes and conspiracy theories, the manifesto was written for a global audience of violent extremists. The focus in this chapter is on the enabling relationship between social media and the rise of contemporary fascism, the so-called 'alt-right'. Social media may not have caused the massacre but it has been central to: (1) shaping an alt-right imaginary in which the 'White Races' face extinction; (2) forging a global brotherhood espousing real-world, violent action; and (3) providing a global forum within which such atrocities may be planned, executed, distributed and consumed. My analysis is situated within the context of the mainstream political discourses of disinformation associated with populist politics, especially of US President Trump, and the monopoly position enjoyed by a small

---

1   Prime Minister Jacinda Ardern requested that the terrorist be nameless in all reports and commentaries on the Christchurch massacre. Her expressed motivation has been to thwart the terrorist's goal of achieving personal fame. In respect of this request, in this chapter, the terrorist is not named in the text although references and quotations that use his name have not been altered (Walquist, 2019).

number of major social media companies. When, on 6 January 2021, Facebook finally banned President Trump from its platform, it had taken the invasion of Congress by a violent mob bent on insurrection to trigger that action.

The Christchurch massacre was a 'made for social media' event, designed to go viral on Facebook and spread rapidly across other platforms. To maximise audience size, the terrorist posted on 8chan that he would livestream the attack, and tweeted hints of the impending massacre. Then, with a GoPro camera strapped to his helmet, the terrorist framed his Facebook livestream to mimic a first-person shooter video game. Centred within the frame, fascist symbols and the names of mass shooters, Serbian war criminals and massacres were scrawled in white paint across his guns. The entire attack, including the drive-time between mosques, featured a soundtrack of martial music and fascist anthems. This livestreaming of mass murder may have been shocking but it was by no means original (Singer and Brooking, 2018). Nor is the idea of 'terrorism as theatre' new, with the phenomenon documented decades before Facebook was even founded (Jenkins, 1974). Rather, social media has amplified terrorist causes and is implicated at every level of its operations. Since 15 March, governments and international forums have focused on reducing the efficacy of social media as a tool for terrorism. Yet, the origins and implications of Christchurch extend far beyond Aotearoa New Zealand, all the way to Washington DC, and move us beyond social media to the fundamental principles and values of Western democracies.

The path to Christchurch

Since the Twin Towers attack of 9/11, Islamist extremism has been the primary focus of terrorism debates and measures in Western nations (Blee, 2016). During the same period, the West has also experienced the rapid rise of alt-right terror attacks by white nationalists. Indeed, the majority of terror attacks in the US itself have been perpetrated by alt-right extremists. Such attacks have been treated differently by Western governments and by the news media, which has tended to frame them as almost inexplicable acts committed by deranged individuals. For example, Britain's *Telegraph* headlined the Christchurch massacre with the headline, 'The "ordinary white man" turned mass murderer' (Ward, 2019), while the *Daily Mirror* described the killer as an 'angelic boy', and both newspapers carried a photo of the terrorist as a towhead child in the arms of his father (Ben Lazreg, 2019). In contrast, attacks by Islamist terrorists are less likely to be attributed to individual pathologies and more likely to be portrayed as the product of extremist ideologies (Blee, 2016). A recent study found that terror attacks by Islamist extremists attract significantly greater news media attention in the West than do those by other perpetrators (Kearns et al., 2019). This differential framing is consistent with the worldview that terror threats in the West are driven by external forces – an 'othering' of perpetrators – which aligns with an increased emphasis on border control. It also aligns with the rhetoric of US President Donald Trump, whose political statements and Twitter posts were marked by anti-Muslim sentiment, such as false claims that thousands of Muslims living in New Jersey had cheered on 9/11 as the Twin Towers came down (MPowerChange.Org, 2019).

President Trump backed his rhetoric with a series of measures to limit or ban Muslims from entering the US. His campaign manager and subsequent head strategist in the White House, Steve Bannon, was the former executive chairman of Breitbart News, a website known for its alt-right, anti-Muslim and anti-immigration content (Heft et al., 2019). In comparison to his consistent stance against Islamist terrorism, President Trump's position on alt-right violence was, at best, ambivalent (Kaiser et al., 2019). Most notably, President Trump declared that there were 'very fine people, on both sides', following the murder of a women protesting against a white supremacist rally in Charlottesville, Virginia (Sparrow, 2018). The rally appears to have been organised in a chat group on the video-gamers' site, Discord. It began on the University of Virginia campus where hundreds marched bearing tiki torches while chanting racist and fascist slogans such as 'Blood and soil', 'White lives matter' and 'You will not replace us' (Kelkar, 2017; Hanna et al., 2017). These same themes feature in the manifesto of the Christchurch terrorist and across the social media sites associated with contemporary fascism. Given the apparent mainstreaming of the alt-right under the Trump administration, the relative inaction of the major online service providers in the face of growing extremism becomes more understandable. For example, the two US social media giants, Facebook and Alphabet (owner of Google and YouTube), have been ongoing targets of criticism by US conservatives for their alleged left-wing bias (Singer and Brooking, 2018; Romm, 2019).

In an environment in which major companies are fearful of a legislative backlash that would hit profitability, the door was opened for alt-right extremism to proliferate across the internet.

The term 'alt-right' was popularised by a 'webzine' created in 2010 by Richard Spencer and is now loosely applied to individuals and groups espousing neo-Nazi, fascist, white nationalist, anti-Semitic, anti-feminist and anti-immigration views. While anti-globalisation is a core theme for the alt-right, the movement itself is globally connected through a network of websites, social media pages and chat spaces. Some of these spaces are on the dark web, which is an encrypted part of the internet and not accessible through search engines. However, much alt-right communication – like the organisation of Charlottesville – is undertaken in plain sight on, for example, Facebook, YouTube and Twitter (Chaudhry and Gruzd, 2019). In their 2018 book, *Like War: The Weaponization of Social Media*, Singer and Brooking (2018, pp. 169–70) argue that:

> As it has with so many other movements, social media has revolutionized white nationalist, white supremacist, and neo-Nazi groups, spiking their membership and allowing their views to move back into mainstream discourse. In the United States, the number of Twitter followers of such groups ballooned 600 per cent between 2012 and 2016, and the Southern Poverty Law Center now tracks some 1,600 far-right extremist groups.

Those who identify with alt-right ideology and causes appear to move between the public internet and dark net, reserving much but by no means all of their most extreme content and hate speech for the latter. This pattern is evident in the reported postings of those who have gone on to commit attacks, including the Christchurch terrorist and the attackers he inspired, in El Paso, Texas, and Poway, California.

The alt-right movement might be characterised as what Bennett and Segerberg (2012, p. 760) have termed a 'connective' rather than a 'collective' network. Connective networks are self-organising across social media platforms and do not require formal membership of organisations. They function as trusted social networks for the sharing of political content that is readily personalised and semantically open, enabling people with a broad range of motivations and levels of commitment to participate. Memes feature strongly in connective networks, representing both a common trope within the community and an opportunity for individual expression. Connective networks therefore provide a space for identity formation and performance. While such networks often celebrate real-world achievements aligned with their core beliefs, there is no expectation that participants will translate their own online engagement into real-world action. Indeed, as will be discussed below, continued tolerance of extremist connective networks is often justified on free speech grounds.

The content that circulates within alt-right networks is a mash-up of facts, lies, conspiracy theories, misinformation, memes and historical analysis (Kaiser et al., 2019). A fresh stream of material that reinforces alt-right ideology and gives it currency is provided by media sites ranging from the partisan *Fox News* to the extremist *Daily Stormer* chat board, which is openly neo-Nazi. In their analysis of the links between these sites, Kaiser and colleagues found that the more extreme the site, the more it was focused on identity-defining issues, such as Islam and immigration (Kaiser et al., 2019). While identity politics are normally associated with the left, the alt-right may also be seen as a form of identity politics (Sparrow, 2018; Stump and Dixit, 2016). Identity politics is centred on the oppression experienced by groups of people based on their characteristics, such as race, gender or sexuality. Core to the identity politics of the alt-right is the belief that the so-called 'white races' are oppressed by multiculturalism and faced with 'extinction' due to immigration and abortion. There is even a core group within the alt-right who label themselves 'incels' or involuntarily celibates, and blame feminism for their inability to find sexual partners. The 'Identitarian' label is now used widely within European alt-right networks, where Muslims are portrayed as an oppressive, invading force to be resisted and pushed back to their own 'homelands' (Ebner, 2017).

Identitarian ideology, which circulates via alt-right social media, is evident throughout the Great Replacement manifesto. This online material was reinforced for the Christchurch terrorist by a self-guided study tour of Asia and Europe, where he learned firsthand about the version of anti-Islamist history promoted by Identitarians. His focus appears to have been on the defeat of the Ottoman Empire, and included visits to the sites of historic battles between Serbians and invading Ottoman armies. He also sought meetings with people active in the European 'Identitarian' movement. His Great Replacement manifesto represents a combination of these real and virtual world experiences, and serves multiple functions including justifying violent action against Muslims, aligning the terrorist with the alt-right and Identitarian politics, and framing the massacre as a political act.

An Australian national, the terrorist migrated to Dunedin in 2017. Aotearoa New Zealand does not seem the logical choice for a person who professed in his Great Replacement manifesto to believe both in white supremacy and in the concept of ethnic groups remaining in their so-called 'homelands'. The country is renowned for its strong commitment to biculturalism based on a partnership between the indigenous Māori and the Crown that originates in the nation's founding document, the Treaty of Waitangi. Moreover, those professing the Muslim faith – the terrorist's primary target – made up only 1 per cent of the population according to the 2013 Census. That same census showed that the largest source of immigrants to Christchurch was England (Stats NZ, 2013). While there is limited information about the terrorist's reasons for choosing Aotearoa New Zealand, it is clear that the country's relatively lax gun laws were a factor. In Dunedin, he was able to legally purchase semi-automatic rifles and practise the rapid firing of multiple rounds at his local gun club. However, the terrorist's goals included maximising the number of Muslim people killed and Dunedin had few Muslim residents (Malley, 2019). In contrast, Christchurch offered three mosques located within easy driving distance. The city also boasted excellent mobile broadband. With the alt-right agenda of taking violent action against Muslim immigrants as the motivating force, the site of the attack may have been less important than the ease with which a large massacre could be carried out and livestreamed through social media.

Livestreaming a massacre

In the days leading up to 15 March, the Christchurch terrorist was active on Facebook, Twitter and 8chan. The 8chan website hosted the notorious /pol/ message board, the home of fascists and white supremacists of all affiliations. It was to this receptive audience that the terrorist made his last 8chan post

> Well lads, it's time to stop sh*tposting[2] and time to make a real life effort post. I will carry out and [sic] attack against the invaders, and will even livestream the attack via facebook. (McBride, 2019)

---

2   Note: 'sh*tposting' is the practice of posting material online – often large quantities of material – that is poor quality and may be offensive. The practice is intended to annoy or provoke those who are not 'in on the joke' and can be used to disrupt online discussions. It is a favoured tool of the alt-right and of internet trolls more generally (Gorman, 2019).

The link to Facebook enabled supporters to watch the massacre live, comment enthusiastically on its progress and, most importantly for the terrorist's purposes, capture the video and post a link to a file-sharing site so that it could go viral once Facebook had removed the footage (Gorman, 2019). According to Facebook Newsroom (2019a), fewer than 200 people watched the livestream video and none of them made a complaint to Facebook or notified the police. It was only after the gunman had been arrested that Facebook received an official police request to remove the video. By this time, multiple copies were in existence and propagated across the internet. Facebook reported thwarting approximately 1.2 million upload attempts and removing 300,000 copies in the first 24 hours. YouTube did not report the total number of uploads but called the attempts 'unprecedented' in scale (Fussell, 2019).

Social media companies rely heavily on users to report objectionable content and employ large workforces devoted to the task of moderating such reports and removing content that violates company policies (Facebook Newsroom, 2019b). The traumatic nature of this work is detailed in a 2018 film, *The Cleaners*, which documents the lives of thousands of lowly paid social media content moderators based in Manila (Wilson, 2018). The documentary highlights the mental health toll on workers who face a daily parade of horrors. In addition to their ever-growing workforce of content moderators, internet safety advisers and counterterrorism experts, social media companies have invested heavily in developing technologies to automatically block, for example, child pornography, suicides, murders, beheadings and terrorist acts from their platforms. Facebook alone claims that its automated systems enabled the removal of more than 26 million pieces of terrorism-related content in the two years to September 2019 (Facebook Newsroom, 2019d). This figure highlights the scale of the problem, and also points to the size of the workforce on the 'other side' of the problem, producing and disseminating extremist content, including through the use of increasingly sophisticated technologies of their own (Singer and Brooking, 2018). Facebook senior executives, including Zuckerberg and Sandberg, have boasted repeatedly of a 99 per cent pre-emptive removal rate of extremist content. More recently, however, whistleblower Frances Haugen has exposed internal Facebook documents suggesting that the actual removal rate may be as low as 5 per cent (Nix and Etter, 2021).

In the face of all the money, technology and human time devoted to preventing such events, the viral success of the Christchurch massacre video – produced using cheap, basic technology by one person – provides a stark illustration of the challenges faced by social media companies. Artificial intelligence (AI) and 'hashing' technology are the main tools available and they are successful in blocking significant amounts of content (Facebook Newsroom, 2019c). 'Hashing' is akin to taking a digital fingerprint of an image or video. When such content violates the policies of a social media company, a hash is added to a database and is used to automatically block future uploads of that content. In mid-2019, YouTube announced that it had loaded more than 200,000 unique hashes into the database that it shares with other major social media platforms (YouTube Official Blog, 2019). While hashing is adept at blocking the automated reloading of images, there are major weaknesses in the technology. The initial upload of any image will not be in the database and it is this upload that must be prevented if the goal is to prevent livestreaming or reposting to other image-sharing sites. Further, any small alteration to an image, such as adding a watermark or making a video of a video, may fool the system into believing it is assessing a different image.

In the case of the Christchurch footage, there was a further technical issue for AI systems: it was framed as a first-person shooter video game, similar to thousands of other games livestreamed on social media every day. It is difficult for AI to tell the difference between simulated slaughter and actual slaughter. Facebook Newsroom (2019a) reported that there was a 'core community of bad actors working together to continually re-upload edited versions of this video in ways designed to defeat our detection'. In total, they detected 800 distinct versions of the Christchurch massacre video. Not all of those who reposted the video were, however, 'bad actors', with users who may have been horrified by its content nonetheless motivated to share the graphic footage. Sharing newsworthy content with friends is, after all, a highly valued activity on social media platforms. Social media algorithms also tend to promote popular content, rendering them the automated allies of propagandists. The underlying logic of the platforms themselves, along with a whole range of technological and human failings, therefore conspired to ensure that the social media goals of the Christchurch terrorist were achieved.

Shaping and sharing an alt-right legend

Despite the efforts of mainstream social media platforms, material from the Christchurch massacre continues to circulate. Online posts give prominence to the number of deaths – the 'kill count' – and to the killer himself, who is portrayed as a hero and inspiration for the alt-right internationally (Evans, 2019). Given that the video mimicked a first-person shooter game, it is not surprising that shortly after the attack, the footage was reworked into a number of actual video games set in mosques. One game offers the Christchurch terrorist, along with Hitler and President Trump, as a possible avatar (Duffy, 2019). Another version, found on Facebook, combined a game with raw footage of the shootings and appears to have been designed to fool the company's AI systems (Keall, 2019). The game reportedly eluded detection for some two months before being removed following an alert from a journalist.

While gamification of the Christchurch massacre is disturbing, albeit predictable, perhaps the more dangerous development is the rapid 'beatification' of the terrorist on the dark web, where, despite being very much alive, he is routinely referred to as a 'saint'. The Poway Synagogue gunman reportedly posted online that the Christchurch terrorist 'was a catalyst for me personally. He showed me that it could be done. And that it needed to be done' (Dearden, 2019a). The following week, a Norwegian gunman also cited the Christchurch terrorist as the inspiring 'saint' behind his failed attack on a mosque (Dearden, 2019a). The perpetrator of the El Paso massacre, in which 18 people were shot in a Walmart store, referenced both the Christchurch gunman and his manifesto in 8chan posts. While the 8chan community embraced and celebrated El Paso, they were openly critical of what one poster termed the gunman's '0 effort manifesto', comparing his four-page document unfavourably with the 87-page, Great Replacement manifesto (Evans, 2019). Christchurch has become both a motivation and a high bar to match for subsequent alt-right terror attacks.

Given the centrality of 8chan as a host for alt-right terrorists in many nations, it is worth exploring how the website was able to continue for so long. The day after El Paso, Evans (2019) posted on the open-source intelligence site, Bellingcat, that:

> In the wake of the Christchurch shooting I published my first
> Bellingcat article about 8chan. I was interviewed by numerous
> media agencies about the website, and I warned all of them
> that additional attacks would follow – every month or two –
> until something was done. This prediction has proven accurate.
> Until law enforcement, and the media, treat these shooters as part
> of a terrorist movement no less organized, or deadly, than ISIS or
> Al Qaeda, the violence will continue. There will be more killers,
> more gleeful celebration of body counts on 8chan, and more
> bloody attempts to beat the last killer's 'high score'.

The ability of 8chan to continue to operate lay in the services, including
crucial protection from DDOS[3] attacks that the site received from the
internet infrastructure company, Cloudflare. After the Christchurch
attack and for two days after El Paso, the company continued to defend
its support of 8chan on the basis that moderating content was not
Cloudflare's responsibility (Wong, 2019). When Cloudflare did drop
8chan as a client, other companies followed suit and the site suspended
services. However, within months it was back, rebranded as '8Kun'
but without the /pol/ message board. Some of the extremist chatter of
/pol/ migrated to the online gamers' chat app, Discord, while the 'dark
libraries' of, for example, Nazi videos, moved to the encrypted messaging
app, Telegram (Glaser, 2019). Prominent on 8Kun are the conspiracy
theories of QAnon, which were lent support by President Trump even
after the FBI had labelled this network a domestic terror threat. The role
and libertarian rhetoric of the network of internet companies that
enable extremist websites and apps to operate will be explored below.
First, however, the multilateral and national responses to Christchurch
are examined.

Multilateral responses

The viral success of the Christchurch massacre amplified existing concerns
about the central role of social media in the spread of violent extremism
online (VEO) and motivated some governments to take further, united
action. In May 2019, Prime Minister Jacinda Ardern joined with French
President Emmanuel Macron to produce the Christchurch Call to

---

3   Distributed denial of service (DDOS) attacks are attempts to disrupt a website by flooding it
with web traffic.

Action, which sought cooperation between governments and technology companies to eliminate VEO. The opening section of the Christchurch Call states:

> The Call outlines collective, voluntary commitments from Governments and online service providers intended to address the issue of terrorist and violent extremist content online and to prevent the abuse of the internet as occurred in and after the Christchurch attacks. All action on this issue must be consistent with principles of a free, open and secure internet, without compromising human rights and fundamental freedoms, including freedom of expression. It must also recognise the internet's ability to act as a force for good, including by promoting innovation and economic development and fostering inclusive societies. (MFAT, 2019)

A central theme within the Christchurch Call – balancing human rights and free speech protections with the prevention of VEO – is evident in this statement. However, citing First Amendment concerns, the US was noticeably absent among the signatories to the call, which included social media giants, Facebook, Twitter and YouTube along with the EU and 17 nations. Subsequently, a further 33 signatories were added to the call, bringing the total number of nations to 47.

A statement released by the US Embassy in New Zealand at the time of the Christchurch Call condemned VEO but asserted:

> We maintain that the best tool to defeat terrorist speech is productive speech, and thus we emphasize the importance of promoting credible, alternative narratives as the primary means by which we can defeat terrorist messaging. (US Embassy and Consulate in New Zealand, 2019)

However, the day after the Christchurch Call was released, the White House released its own call, which appeared to move in the opposite direction. Through the White House Twitter account, @WhiteHouse, users were invited to submit details of instances in which they had been 'censored or silenced online'. This invitation built on allegations made two weeks earlier by Donald Trump Junior of a left-wing bias on social media, including in the following Twitter post:

The purposeful & calculated silencing of conservatives by @facebook & the rest of the Big Tech monopoly men should terrify everyone.

It appears they're taking their censorship campaign to the next level.

Ask yourself, how long before they come to purge you? We must fight back. (Trump Jr, 2019)

This post followed the decision taken by Facebook, as part of its stated commitment to removing hate speech, to place a permanent ban on the alt-right conspiracy site, InfoWars, and on the pages of several prominent figures associated with hate groups.

Despite its subject matter, the Christchurch Call is a softly worded document that contains specific, though non-binding, commitments by governments and online service providers to work individually and collectively to combat VEO. While the primary focus is on the internet, it is noteworthy that the first government commitment relates not to the internet but to social cohesion: 'Counter the drivers of terrorism and violent extremism by strengthening the resilience and inclusiveness of our societies to enable them to resist terrorist and extremist ideologies'. This statement reflects the actions of Prime Minister Ardern who was widely praised when she asked that the nation come together in support of the Muslim community. When President Trump called to offer his condolences and ask what assistance the US might provide, Prime Minister Ardern reportedly asked that he demonstrate 'sympathy and love for all Muslim communities' (Cooke, 2019).

One month after the Christchurch Call, the G20 (2019, Japan) issued a multilateral statement of its own, the 'G20 Osaka Leaders' Statement on Preventing Exploitation of the Internet for Terrorism and Violent Extremism Conducive to Terrorism'. Although the G20 statement did not differ substantially from the Christchurch Call in its balancing of free speech and VEO limitations, this time the US was a party to the statement. The US involvement may be due to other differences between the two documents. The G20 statement is shorter, at just 578 words compared with the Christchurch Call's 1,376 words, and much less specific in relation to the commitments of governments themselves, while 'urging' action on the part of online platforms. Perhaps the most notable difference, however, is that the G20 statement makes no mention of the need for governments to work on community 'inclusivity' or social cohesion as a key strategy for combating terrorism. Rather, the G20 statement places responsibility for action onto the major internet companies.

In addition to the multilateral responses embodied in the Christchurch Call and the G20 statement, there have been a number of unilateral actions by nations concerned with regulating the impact of the internet on their societies. The actions of the two nations arguably most affected by Christchurch – Aotearoa New Zealand, the site of the massacre, and Australia, its nearest neighbour and country of citizenship for the terrorist – are briefly outlined below, followed by an overview of industry responses.

National responses: Aotearoa New Zealand

There are four main strands to Aotearoa New Zealand's domestic response to Christchurch: increasing gun control; emphasising the inclusivity of society; preventing the spread of VEO through improving the policies, practices and technologies of online service providers, especially social media companies; and assessing the performance of state agencies in light of the attack. Within 72 hours of the massacre, the government announced plans to tighten the nation's relatively lax gun control laws. Legislation to ban military-style semi-automatics and assault rifles was passed three weeks later by an overwhelming majority of 119 to one. This rare, united stance of parliament reflects a broader national unity that followed the attack. In her speech to the National Remembrance Service, themed as 'We Are One', Prime Minister Ardern spoke of the collective responsibility to combat hate by embracing the humanity of all people (Ardern, 2019a).

While the immediate focus for Aotearoa New Zealand was dealing with the aftermath of the massacre, there was recognition that the context for the attack extended well beyond national borders. Prime Minister Ardern expressed the view that addressing the complexities of VEO would require collaboration within and between multiple nations and across multiple sectors:

> In the wake of the March 15 attacks New Zealanders united in common purpose to ensure such attacks never occur again. If we want to prevent violent extremist content online we need to take a global approach that involves other governments, tech companies and civil society leaders. (Ardern, 2019b)

This 'global approach' took the form of the Christchurch Call discussed above. It also led Aotearoa New Zealand to work with the Global Internet Forum to Counter Terrorism (GIFCT), an existing consortium founded by Facebook, Microsoft, Twitter and YouTube. Through GIFCT, major online service companies shared knowledge of terrorist activities, collaborated on the development of technologies to combat VEO and undertook joint research. Following the Christchurch Call, and citing it as its inspiration, GIFCT took the further step of becoming an independent agency with an enlarged remit to work in collaboration with civil society and government stakeholders (GIFCT, 2019).

Aotearoa New Zealand's vehicle for assessing the role of state agencies in relation to the massacre took the form of a Royal Commission of Inquiry. The focus of the Royal Commission was on state agencies and it was tasked with identifying ways of reducing the likelihood of future attacks. Following release of the Royal Commission's report in December 2020, Prime Minister Ardern apologised for failings on the part of intelligence agencies, which, like those in other Western nations, had failed to pay appropriate attention to right-wing extremism. Subsequently, the government established an Office for Ethnic Communities, appointed a minister for inclusion, diversity and ethnic communities inside Cabinet, launched a new police program to combat hate crime and criminalised the planning of a terrorist attack.

National responses: Australia

For Australia, the Christchurch massacre represented the nation's first experience of having exported alt-right terrorism to a close ally. Mirroring the US example discussed above, the Australian Government's discourse on terrorist threats had, since 9/11, centred on Islamist extremist groups with relatively little attention paid to the alt-right. Given the exceptional nature of the massacre, the nationality and ideology of the terrorist might have seemed a natural new focus of attention for Australia. Instead, at least from an Australian Government perspective, attention has been directed to the US-based social media companies. On the day of the massacre, Australian Prime Minister Scott Morrison spoke of mounting a joint counterterrorism operation with Aotearoa New Zealand in acknowledgement of the fact that the perpetrator was an 'Australian-born citizen' and a 'right-wing extremist, violent terrorist' (PM of Australia Media Centre, 2019a). However, mention of the terrorist's Australian nationality or of right-wing extremism quickly disappeared from Prime Minister Morrison's statements. Just two weeks after the massacre, when the Prime Minister was attending the National Remembrance Service in Aotearoa New Zealand, he went so far as to deny that the terrorist should be regarded as Australian in the following exchange with a journalist:

> Journalist: Is there a sense of guilt, a sense of responsibility [inaudible] given that the [inaudible] Australian citizen?
>
> Prime Minister: The crime was perpetuated by an extremist terrorist and extremist terrorists have no nationality. (PM of Australia Media Centre, 2019b)

Other than in his initial statements, Prime Minister Morrison consistently framed the export of terrorism as a failure not of Australia but of social media companies, and as a problem best addressed by technological solutions. He spoke of 'calling out social media companies on their responsibilities', asserting that:

> They have a responsibility when they put these platforms into public use, to make sure they are safe and that they cannot be weaponised by terrorists. Similarly, they shouldn't be able to be weaponised for other forms of harm that can affect the youngest of us around here today, through to the most serious of criminal offences. (PM of Australia Media Centre, 2019c)

Prime Minister Morrison also suggested that the problem was a lack of will or commitment to action by the social media companies:

> If they can write an algorithm to make sure that the ads they want you to see can appear on your mobile phone, then I'm quite confident they can write an algorithm to screen out hate content on social media platforms. (Laschon and Dalzell, 2019)

In line with this framing, and just three weeks after Christchurch, an *Amendment to the Criminal Code* regarding the 'Sharing of Abhorrent Violent Material' was rushed through both houses of parliament.

The amendment, which is analysed in detail in Chapter 6, was aimed at holding internet service providers, content service providers and hosting service providers accountable for abhorrent material (Keller, 2019).

The Criminal Code Amendment was immediately and widely criticised, including by the UN special rapporteur on the promotion and protection of the right to freedom of opinion and expression, and by the UN special rapporteur on the promotion and protection of human rights and fundamental freedoms while countering terrorism. In a joint letter to the Australian minister for foreign affairs, the rapporteurs expressed doubt over the amendment's apparent faith in unproven technological solutions, which might lead companies to adopt a heavy-handed approach in order to avoid significant penalties. They also expressed:

> Serious concerns that the approach, particularly the haste of presentation and adoption of the legislation and key elements of the Law itself, unduly interferes with Australia's obligations under international human rights law. (Kaye and Ní Aoláin, 2019)

Legal academic Nicola McGarrity has speculated that the Australian tendency to resort to restrictive legislation may be due to a lack of constitutionally enshrined, free speech protection:

> Australia is the only country in the western democratic world that lacks a national constitutional or statutory bill of rights, and that has meant where other countries exercise restraint because they're unsure whether measures will impact on freedom of speech or freedom of association or the right to privacy … Australia can just adopt a really gung-ho approach. (Burgess, 2019)

Regardless, the rapporteurs' concerns were dismissed by the Australian ambassador and permanent representative to the UN on a number of grounds, including that the scope of the legislation was very narrow and that it was necessary to limit the sharing of 'abhorrent violent material' that 'can threaten national security, perpetuate further criminal activity, prejudice the dignity of victims and has the potential to cause harm and distress to various sections of the community' (Mansfield, 2019). Subsequently, there has been limited explanation of how the legislation will operate in practice and no additional resources have as yet been announced in support of its enactment.

In addition to pushing through legislation at home, Prime Minister Morrison called for the upcoming G20 meeting to discuss social media governance, which resulted in the G20 Osaka Leaders Statement described above. He also convened an Australian summit with major digital platforms, internet service providers and government agencies and ministers, which established the Australian Taskforce to Combat Terrorist and Extreme Violent Material Online. Reporting on 21 June, the taskforce recommended a series of voluntary measures for industry action, including in collaboration with the GIFCT and Australian Government agencies (ATCTEVMO, 2019). These measures included 'proactive technical intervention', 'enhanced moderation' and 'live-streaming controls' along with 'periodic reporting' by industry to government. The taskforce report also partially addressed the enlarged role of Australia's eSafety commissioner who, following the passage of the Criminal Code Amendment, had found her remit expanded from cyber bullying of children and 'image-based abuse' of adults, to combating terrorism. This sudden pivot, from cybersafety to cybersecurity, enlarges the remit of the commissioner quite significantly, and in ways that may overlap or conflict with the remit of national security agencies.

Industry responses

In livestreaming the Christchurch massacre, Facebook unintentionally placed a large spotlight on itself and the governance, reach and influence of internet companies more generally. Arguably, the industry has achieved its phenomenal success partly because the regulatory and policy environments within which it operates were designed before it was invented and are ill-suited to its governance. In the wide spaces between the rules, Facebook has grown from a rather disreputable website run out of Mark Zuckerberg's student dorm, into a Fortune 500 corporation with around 2.4 billion users and annual revenues exceeding US$60 billion. In the absence of externally imposed rules, companies like Facebook have made up their own, often on an ad hoc basis and in response to a new crisis or scandal. The many gaps in the self-regulation of internet companies is partly due to the speed of their development. However, from the very beginning these companies have been highly resistant to the imposition of regulation or any oversight by governments. Instead, the unprecedented rise of the major internet companies, from startups to globally dominant, multinational corporations, has occurred in the context of a strongly libertarian internet culture.

Since the launch of the World Wide Web, when the internet became available to individuals and the private sector, key figures in the internet's development have been critical of any form of government control. For example, in his oft-quoted *Declaration of the Independence of Cyberspace*, a co-founder of the Electronic Frontier Foundation, John Perry Barlow (1996), declared:

> Governments of the Industrial World, you weary giants of flesh and steel, I come from Cyberspace, the new home of Mind. On behalf of the future, I ask you of the past to leave us alone … I declare the global social space we are building to be naturally independent of the tyrannies you seek to impose on us. You have no moral right to rule us nor do you possess any methods of enforcement we have true reason to fear.

Their utopian vision for the World Wide Web was of an anarchic, global paradise of individual freedom. This vision was blown apart in 2013 by the revelations of whistleblower Edward Snowden who revealed the extent to which internet traffic was being monitored by the US Government (Motion et al., 2016). Since then, there have been multiple instances in which the internet has been harnessed for the surveillance and manipulation of whole populations by state and criminal actors. Rather than being a domain of individual freedom, the internet has been systematically walled off, concentrated and privatised by a small number of companies who have emerged as a new form of monopoly capitalism and market failure. As governments have sought to gain control over the internet, especially in areas related to national security, taxation and crime, its international character has been compromised by increasing fragmentation along national boundaries, most notably by China and North Korea (Singer and Brooking, 2018).

Public trust in the major internet companies was further damaged by their role in the 2016 US presidential election. Following the surprise defeat of Hillary Clinton, Facebook was found to be the source of personal data used illegally by British political consulting firm Cambridge Analytica in support of the Trump campaign, including with so-called 'fake news' posts (Margetts, 2019). Facebook also sold advertising to a Russian-based 'troll factory', the Internet Research Agency, which was later indicted by a US

Grand Jury on charges of interfering with a US election. Facebook first denied, then downplayed, the possibility that misuse of its platform could play a significant role in voter choices. By late 2017, Facebook was under such pressure that CEO Zuckerberg backtracked from his earlier position, and admitted that it was not 'a crazy idea' that the scale of the platform was such that it might be deployed to change the outcome of an election (Levin, 2017).

The view that major social media platforms might be 'weaponised' by bad actors for political and criminal purposes took hold. After an extensive investigation by the US Federal Trade Commission (FTC) into the misuse of the private data of 87 million users, Facebook was fined US$5 billion. This statement by the FTC chairman highlights the extent of alleged wrongdoing in relation to data privacy:

> In 2012, Facebook entered into a consent order with the FTC, resolving allegations that the company misrepresented to consumers the extent of data sharing with third-party applications and the control consumers had over that sharing ... Our complaint announced today alleges that Facebook failed to live up to its commitments under that order. Facebook subsequently made similar misrepresentations about sharing consumer data with third-party apps and giving users control over that sharing, and misrepresented steps certain consumers needed to take to control [over] facial recognition technology. Facebook also allowed financial considerations to affect decisions about how it would enforce its platform policies against third-party users of data, in violation of its obligation under the 2012 order to maintain a reasonable privacy program. In addition to these order violations, today's complaint alleges that Facebook violated the FTC Act by engaging in a new set of deceptive practices relating to the collection and use of consumer phone numbers provided by consumers to enable security features such as two-factor authentication. (USFTC, 2019)

The FTC statement alleges that internet companies cannot be relied upon to voluntarily 'do the right thing' in the absence of legal constraints and in the face of significant and conflicting financial incentives. More than this, the statement alleges both 'misrepresentations' and 'deceptive practices' in relation to data privacy, which suggests active intent rather than accidental violations.

The Snowden revelations and the FTC judgement had focused public attention on data privacy and data protection. The Christchurch massacre raised a whole new set of concerns centred on the lack of accountability by internet companies for the content posted by users, with an additional level of concern in relation to the livestreaming of atrocities. In the US, s. 230 of the Communications Decency Act of 1996 protects internet companies from any responsibility for the content posted by users (Harvard Law Review, 2018). For example, Zeran v. America Online, Inc. found that s. 230 'creates a federal immunity to any cause of action that would make service providers liable for information originating with a third party user of the service' (Harvard Law Review, 2018). Under s. 230, internet platforms have enjoyed legally immunity from prosecution – at least in the US – for the publication of prohibited forms of speech, including defamation. Indeed, despite becoming the world's largest publishers of content and gatekeepers to the content of others, Facebook and Alphabet have not been legally defined as publishers at all. At the time of writing, and following the storming of the US Capitol Building by a mob intent on preventing the confirmation of President Biden, a Bill that would place limits on s. 230 is before the US Congress. Outside the US, governments have also begun to hold internet companies responsible for their user-generated content, including through the Australian *Amendment to the Criminal Code* discussed above and in subsequent chapters by Wheeler and by Nolan and Dalla-Pozza.

In the face of growing pressure to act, the major internet companies have been active participants in global discussions around combating VEO, including becoming signatories to the Christchurch Call. The arguments of the libertarian past have been all but abandoned as companies struggle to deal with the attempted invasion of their platforms by a myriad of bad actors including terrorists, paedophiles, fraudsters and troll farms propagating 'fake news' (Coleman, 2015). Two weeks after Christchurch, Facebook CEO, Zuckerberg, stated:

> Every day we make decisions about what speech is harmful, what constitutes political advertising, and how to prevent sophisticated cyberattacks. These are important for keeping our community safe. But if we were starting from scratch, we wouldn't ask companies to make these judgments alone. I believe we need a more active role for governments and regulators. By updating the rules for the internet, we can preserve what's best about it – the freedom for people to express themselves and for entrepreneurs

to build new things – while also protecting society from broader harms. From what I've learned, I believe we need new regulation in four areas: harmful content, election integrity, privacy and data portability. (Kimball, 2019)

The statement both invites government intervention and attempts to steer the attention of governments and regulators in particular directions. As discussed above, the major social media platforms are already spending billions on voluntary content moderation, and on safety and security more generally. One of the biggest threats these companies face to their global business model is the increasing 'balkanisation' of the internet that is occurring in response to, for example, terror attacks and foreign interference in elections. After self-regulation in an environment of zero liability for their content, the next best option for internet companies would be globally agreed rules that they had had a major role in drafting.

Being seen to act as good and concerned corporate citizens is also a defensive strategy in the face of an additional threat to the business model of the major players, such as Facebook, Alphabet and Amazon. In an opinion piece entitled 'It's time to break up Facebook', the company's co-founder, Chris Hughes (2019), argued that: 'Facebook isn't afraid of a few more rules. It's afraid of an antitrust case and of the kind of accountability that real government oversight would bring'. The sheer size and reach of platforms such as Facebook, Google, YouTube and Twitter underpins their profitably. It also enhances their utility for fraudsters, terrorists, election hackers and other bad actors. In the face of numerous scandals and crises, such as the livestreaming of the Christchurch massacre, governments are under increasing pressure to address the growing power of the major internet companies.

In July 2019, the US Department of Justice announced that it was 'reviewing whether and how market-leading online platforms have achieved market power and are engaging in practices that have reduced competition, stifled innovation, or otherwise harmed consumers' (USDoJ, 2019). A month earlier, the Australian Competition and Consumer Commission (ACCC) had released its own *Digital Platforms Inquiry*, which focused on the detrimental impacts of major platforms on conventional news media. Despite the fact that they do not produce news, and are therefore exempt from the complex regulatory frameworks governing media companies, Facebook and Google emerged as major players in the Australian news media market (ACCC, 2019, p. 101). Advertising revenues have shifted accordingly, leading to the reduced production of Australian news content by cash-strapped media companies. The ACCC found that such news was 'important for the healthy functioning of the democratic process' and that there was no evidence of a 'business model that can effectively replace the advertiser model' for media companies (p. 1). A new 'platform-neutral regularity framework' that would level the playing field was recommended (p. 31). This recommendation is in sharp contrast with the s. 230 protections and advantages enjoyed by internet companies in the US.

The ACCC inquiry found that 'disinformation', which was widespread on the major platforms, was being used to 'influence public opinion', and was a 'significant public policy concern' (ACCC, 2019, p. 358). In the interests of protecting Australian democracy, the ACCC recommended a raft of measures to address the perceived market failure, including increased funding for public broadcasters and for media literacy programs in schools and the broader community. While finding evidence that the algorithms deployed by major digital platforms tended to direct users to increasingly extreme content, the ACCC concluded that more research was required to understand 'echo chambers' effects. They did not make any specific recommendations in relation to the role of social media in the radicalisation of terrorists or the creation of a more divided polity. At the time of writing, a Bill is before the Australian Parliament that would require Google and Facebook to pay Australian media for the use of their content. Given that the Bill could potentially set a global precedent, it has been met with fierce opposition from Google, which has threatened to turn off its 'search' function, and Facebook, which has threatened to block Australian content.

The lessons of Christchurch

Despite all the media attention, agreements signed and commitments to action made by governments and industry since Christchurch, there have been multiple copycat attacks by suspected alt-right terrorists. One such attack, on a German synagogue, was livestreamed on Amazon's Twitch without any human or AI intervention, and the video was subsequently shared across multiple platforms (Haselton and Graham, 2019). As with Christchurch, the shooter had posted a hate-filled manifesto outlining his white nationalist ideology, this time on the German-language site, Kohlchan (Dearden, 2019b). On other extremist sites, the attack is already being celebrated in the name of the 'sainted' Christchurch terrorist.

Amazon is a signatory to the Christchurch Call, including to the pledge to implement 'immediate, effective measures to mitigate the specific risk that terrorist and violent extremist content is disseminated through livestreaming' (MFAT, 2019). The major lesson to be learned from the Christchurch massacre may be the confronting reality of how difficult it is to prevent the attacks themselves along with their global dissemination through social media. However, internet platforms play a far broader role than that of mere broadcasters. They appear to be implicated in multiple, overlapping ways, including as a contributing cause and source of motivation for terror attacks. The platforms have become a standard part of the terrorist's toolkit for marketing ideology, recruiting followers, advertising successful massacres and canonising perpetrators. Through social media, the alt-right has become a globally connected community, united against perceived threats to the dominance of white men. Feminists, Muslims, Jews and refugees are all targets of their hate speech. The Christchurch terrorist and his imitators all used social media to encourage direct, violent action against these targets. Social media did not cause the terrorists to embrace extremism in any straightforward way, but it did provide a community of like-minded people who reinforced the validity of mass murder in the name of white nationalism. The community furnished role models to emulate and provided advice on terror methodology. A helmet-mounted camera with an internet connection is now a key part of this methodology. In short, social media figures in every aspect of the Christchurch terror attack: in its inspiration, planning, preparation and execution, and in perpetuating its iconic status within the alt-right community.

This chapter has outlined some of the responses to Christchurch on the part of governments and industry that were intended to prevent future massacres. Unfortunately, these responses have raised a myriad of related, complex issues that reduce the likelihood that the responses will succeed. From the start, government statements on the massacre emphasised the importance of an inclusive society that embraced Muslims. However, this framing conflicted with the mainstream media's portrayal of Muslims as a source (not a target) of terrorism (Blee, 2016). It also conflicted with the discourse of US President Trump who was elected on a platform that resonated with alt-right fears of immigration and Islamist terror.

This mainstreaming of alt-right ideas was reinforced by President Trump when he rejected the Christchurch Call, and by Donald Trump Jr who openly attacked the so-called 'Big Tech monopoly men' on the basis that they endangered 'conservatives' (Trump Jr, 2019). The word 'monopoly' played directly to the biggest fear of major internet companies, which is an antitrust suit that would lead to their dismantling. Much of the delicate work of blocking or countering extremist content while not impinging on free speech falls to US-based multinationals, such as Facebook, Alphabet and Amazon. The companies are seriously conflicted in making these fine judgements by their desire to avoid offending those capable of threatening their market dominance.

Internet companies are not alone in their struggle to balance free speech with internet safety. The Australian Government faced this same dilemma when it amended the Criminal Code to make internet companies liable if they failed to remove 'abhorrent violent material' swiftly from their platforms. The legislation was criticised for incentivising internet companies to engage in heavy-handed censorship in order to avoid hefty penalties. Australia is signatory to a number of international agreements that would seem to prohibit such censorship. The spectre rises of China's digital Great Wall, which protects citizens from terrorist propaganda but also isolates them from ideas and information not sanctioned by the state. Each fresh tragedy lends further impetus to calls for the erosion of human rights in the name of safety. Technology features in all these debates both as a problem to be solved and as the solution.

The inability of technology, at least in its current phase of development, to perform the tasks we now ask of it is evident. The Australian prime minister was mistaken in his view that automating terrorism detection was akin to automating an advertising feed in social media. Only in the former is the tolerance for errors set at zero due to the massive consequences of mistakes. Even one livestreamed massacre is a catastrophe. While they work on technological solutions, internet companies default to employing thousands of staff dedicated to content moderation. This private army engages in daily battle with terrorists and criminals – driven by a range of ideological and economic motivations – as well with individual hackers who view the battle as sport (Gorman, 2019). Its very existence raises issues of where the public–private divide ought to sit between industry self-governance and government regulation and policing. When individual governments decide to act alone their options are limited by the global character of the internet. When they seek international cooperation, the resulting agreements tend to default to voluntary industry compliance. Meanwhile, the internet itself is a continuously shapeshifting entity that grows in power and reach every day. There are no simple solutions to combating violent extremism online and the complexity is only increasing.

References

ACCC. (2019, June). *Digital Platforms Inquiry: Final Report.* Retrieved from www.accc.gov.au/publications/digital-platforms-inquiry-final-report.

Ardern, J. (2019a, 29 March). *Prime Minister's Speech at the National Remembrance Service.* Retrieved from www.beehive.govt.nz/release/prime-minister%E2% 80%99s-speech-national-remembrance-service.

Ardern, J. (2019b, 24 April). *NZ and France Seek to End Use of Social Media for Acts of Terrorism.* Retrieved from www.beehive.govt.nz/release/nz-and-france-seek-end-use-social-media-acts-terrorism.

ATCTEVMO. (2019, 21 June). *Report of the Australian Taskforce to Combat Terrorist and Extreme Violent Material Online.* Retrieved from www.pmc. gov.au/resource-centre/national-security/report-australian-taskforce-combat-terrorist-and-extreme-violent-material-online.

Barlow, J. P. (1996, 8 February). *A Declaration of the Independence of Cyberspace.* Electronic Frontier Foundation. Retrieved from www.eff.org/cyberspace-independence.

Ben Lazreg, H. (2019, 26 March). The hypocritical media coverage of the New Zealand Terror Attacks. *Conversation.* Retrieved from theconversation.com/ the-hypocritical-media-coverage-of-the-new-zealand-terror-attacks-113713.

Bennett, W. L. & Segerberg, A. (2012). The logic of connective action: Digital media and the personalization of contentious politics. *Information, Communication & Society*, 15 (5), 739–68. doi.org/10.1080/1369118x.2012. 670661.

Blee, K. (2016). Manufacturing fear: Muslim Americans and the politics of terrorism. *Contemporary Sociology*, 45(1), 6–9. Retrieved from www.jstor.org/ stable/43997380.

Burgess, K. (2019, 19 July). Innocent bystanders are increasingly being impacted Australia's national security laws. *Canberra Times.* Retrieved from www. canberratimes.com.au/story/6256747/is-the-government-watching-you/.

Chaudhry, I. & Gruzd, A. (2019). Expressing and challenging racist discourse on Facebook: How social media weaken the 'spiral of silence' theory. *Policy & Internet, Early View.* doi.org/10.1002/poi3.197.

Coleman, G. (2015). *Hacker, Hoaxer, Whistleblower, Spy: The Many Faces of Anonymous.* London: Verso.

Cooke, H. (2019, 16 March). PM Jacinda Ardern told Donald Trump: Send love to Muslims after mosque shooting. *Stuff.* Retrieved from www.stuff.co.nz/national/politics/111331484/pm-jacinda-ardern-told-donald-trump-send-love-to-muslims-after-mosque-shooting.

Dearden, L. (2019a, 24 August). Revered as a saint by online extremists, how Christchurch shooter inspired copycat terrorists around the world. *Independent.* Retrieved from www.independent.co.uk/news/world/australasia/brenton-tarrant-christchurch-shooter-attack-el-paso-norway-poway-a9076926.html.

Dearden, L. (2019b, 10 October). Stephan Balliet: The 'loser' neo-Nazi suspected of deadly attack on German synagogue. *Independent.* Retrieved from www.independent.co.uk/news/world/europe/german-synagogue-shooting-halle-attack-latest-stephan-balliet-suspect-neo-nazi-a9150451.html.

Duffy, N. (2019, 2 June). 'Sick' far-right video game lets people play as Christchurch mosque shooter, Hitler and Trump. *Inews.* Retrieved from inews.co.uk/culture/gaming/sick-far-right-video-game-lets-people-play-as-christchurch-mosque-shooter-hitler-and-trump-501093.

Ebner, J. (2017). *The Rage: The Vicious Circle of Islamist and Far-Right Extremism.* London: I. B. Tauris. doi.org/10.5040/9781350989184.

Evans, R. (2019, 4 August). The El Paso shooting and the gamification of terror. *bellingcat.com.* Retrieved from www.bellingcat.com/news/americas/2019/08/04/the-el-paso-shooting-and-the-gamification-of-terror/.

Facebook Newsroom. (2019a, 20 March). A further update on New Zealand terrorist attack. Retrieved from about.fb.com/news/2019/03/technical-update-on-new-zealand/.

Facebook Newsroom. (2019b, 27 March). Standing against hate. Retrieved from about.fb.com/news/2019/03/standing-against-hate/.

Facebook Newsroom. (2019c, 15 June). Hard questions: How we counter terrorism. Retrieved from about.fb.com/news/2017/06/how-we-counter-terrorism/.

Facebook Newsroom. (2019d, 17 September). Combating hate and extremism. Retrieved from about.fb.com/news/2019/09/combating-hate-and-extremism/.

Fussell, S. (2019, 20 March). Why the New Zealand shooting video keeps circulating. *Atlantic*. Retrieved from www.theatlantic.com/technology/archive/2019/03/facebook-youtube-new-zealand-tragedy-video/585418/.

G20 2019 Japan. (2019). *G20 Osaka Leaders' Statement on Preventing Exploitation of the Internet for Terrorism and Violent Extremism Conducive to Terrorism (VECT)*. Retrieved from www.mofa.go.jp/policy/economy/g20_summit/osaka19/en/documents/final_g20_statement_on_preventing_terrorist_and_vect.html.

GIFCT. (2019). *Global Internet Forum to Counter Terrorism: Evolving an Institution*. Retrieved from gifct.org/about/.

Glaser, A. (2019, 11 November). Where 8channers went after 8chan. *Slate*. Retrieved from slate.com/technology/2019/11/8chan-8kun-white-supremacists-telegram-discord-facebook.html.

Gorman, G. (2019). *Troll Hunting: Inside the World of Online Hate and its Human Fallout*. Melbourne: Hardie Grant Books.

Hanna, J., Hartung, H. J., Sayers, D. M. & Almasy, S. (2017, 13 August). Virginia governor to white nationalists: 'Go home … shame on you'. *CNN.com*. Retrieved from edition.cnn.com/2017/08/12/us/charlottesville-white-nationalists-rally/index.html.

Harvard Law Review. (2018, 10 May). Note: Section 230 as First Amendment rule. *Harvard Law Review*, 131(7), 2027–48. Retrieved from harvardlawreview.org/2018/05/section-230-as-first-amendment-rule/.

Haselton, T. & Graham, M. (2019, 9 October). About 2,200 people watched the German synagogue shooting on Amazon's Twitch. *CNBC*. Retrieved from www.cnbc.com/2019/10/09/the-german-synagogue-shooting-was-streamed-on-twitch.html.

Heft, A., Mayerhoffer, E., Reinharst, S. & Knupfer, C. (2019). Beyond Breitbart: Comparing right-wing digital news infrastructure in six Western democracies. *Policy & Internet*, Early View. doi.org/10.1002/poi3.219.

Hughes, C. (2019, 9 May). It's time to break up Facebook. *New York Times*. Retrieved from www.nytimes.com/2019/05/09/opinion/sunday/chris-hughes-facebook-zuckerberg.html.

Jenkins, B. M. (1974). *International Terrorism: A New Kind of Warfare*. Santa Monica, CA: The Rand Paper Series. Retrieved from www.rand.org/pubs/papers/P5261.html.

Kaiser, J., Rauchfleisch, A. & Bourassa, N. (2019). Connecting the (far-) right dots: A topic modeling and hyperlink analysis of (far-) right media coverage during the US elections. 2016. *Digital Journalism*. doi.org/10.1080/216708 11.2019.1682629.

Kaye, D. & Ní Aoláin, F. (2019, 4 April). *Amendment to the Criminal Code on Sharing of Abhorrent Violent Content, OL AUS 5/2019*. Retrieved from www. ohchr.org/EN/Issues/FreedomOpinion/Pages/LegislationAndPolicy.aspx.

Keall, C. (2019, 23 May). Christchurch massacre game, including shooting footage, found on Facebook. *New Zealand Herald*. Retrieved from www. nzherald.co.nz/business/news/article.cfm?c_id=3&objectid=12233539.

Kearns, E. M., Betus, A. E. & Lemieux, A. F. (2019). Why do some terrorist attacks receive more media attention than others? *Justice Quarterly*, 36:6, 985–1022. doi.org/10.1080/07418825.2018.1524507.

Kelkar, K. (2017, 2 August). Three dead after white nationalist rally in Charlottesville. *PBS.com*. Retrieved from www.pbs.org/newshour/amp/nation/ state-emergency-charlottesville-va-fights-erupt-white-nationalist-rally.

Keller, D. (2019, 11 April). Australia shows the world how not to regulate platforms, news, and public information. The Center for Internet and Society at Stanford Law School. Retrieved from cyberlaw.stanford.edu/ blog/2019/04/australia-shows-world-how-not-regulate-platforms-news-and- public-information.

Kimball, S. (2019, 30 March). Zuckerberg backs stronger internet privacy and election laws: 'We need a more active role for governments'. *CNBC news report*. Retrieved from www.cnbc.com/2019/03/30/mark-zuckerberg-calls-for-tighter- internet-regulations-we-need-a-more-active-role-for-governments.html.

Laschon, E. & Dalzell, S. (2019, 19 March). Scott Morrison wants crackdown on social media companies after sharing of Christchurch shootings footage. *ABC News*. Retrieved from www.abc.net.au/news/2019-03-19/scott-morrison- social-media-companies-christchurch-shootings/10915246.

Levin, S. (2017, 28 September). Mark Zuckerberg: I regret ridiculing fears over Facebook's effect on election. *Guardian*. Retrieved from www.theguardian.com/ technology/2017/sep/27/mark-zuckerberg-facebook-2016-election-fake-news.

McBride, J. (2019, 15 March). Brenton Tarrant social media: Twitter rants, live video. *Heavy.com*. Retrieved from heavy.com/news/2019/03/brenton-tarrant- social-media-twitter-video/.

Malley, P. (2019, 9 September). How many did I kill? Christchurch killer asks police. *Australian*. Retrieved from www.theaustralian.com.au/nation/how-many-did-i-kill-christchurch-killer-asks-police/news-story/23d995df913b66 17cdf86af3604467a1.

Mansfield, S. (2019, 23 September). *Government Reply*. Retrieved from www. ohchr.org/EN/Issues/FreedomOpinion/Pages/LegislationAndPolicy.aspx.

Margetts, H. (2019). Rethinking democracy with social media. In A. Gamble & T. Wright. (Eds). *Rethinking Democracy* (pp. 107–23). Oxford, UK: Wiley.

MFAT. (2019). *The Call*. Retrieved from www.christchurchcall.com/.

Motion, J., Heath, R. L. & Leitch, S. (2016). *Social Media and Public Relations: Fake Friends and Powerful Publics*. Oxford, UK and NY, NY: Routledge. doi.org/10.4324/9780203727799.

MPowerChange.Org. (2019, 18 April). 86 times Donald Trump displayed or promoted Islamophobia. *Medium.com*. Retrieved from medium.com/nilc/86-times-donald-trump-displayed-or-promoted-islamophobia-49e67584ac10.

Nix, N. & Etter, L. (2021, 25 October). Facebook privately worried about hate speech spawning violence. Bloomberg. Retrieved from www.bloomberg.com/news/articles/2021-10-25/facebook-s-fb-hate-speech-problem-worried-its-own-analysts.

Prime Minister of Australia Media Centre. (2019a, 15 March). *Transcript: Live Cross, Seven News*. Retrieved from www.pmtranscripts.pmc.gov.au.

Prime Minister of Australia Media Centre. (2019b, 29 March). *Transcript: Christchurch Doorstop*. Retrieved from www.pmtranscripts.pmc.gov.au.

Prime Minister of Australia Media Centre. (2019c, 30 March). *Transcript: Penrith, NSW, Doorstop*. Retrieved from www.pmtranscripts.pmc.gov.au.

Romm, T. (2019, 11 July). Trump accuses social media companies of 'terrible bias' at White House summit decried by critics. *The Washington Post*. Retrieved from www.washingtonpost.com/technology/2019/07/11/we-will-not-let-them-get-away-with-it-trump-threatens-social-media-ahead-white-house-summit/.

Singer, P. W. & Brooking, E. T. (2018). *LikeWar: The Weaponization of Social Media*. NY, NY: Houghton Mifflin Harcourt Publishing Co.

Sparrow, J. (2018). *Trigger Warnings: Political Correctness and the Rise of the Right*. Melbourne: Scribe.

Stats NZ Tatauranga Aotearoa. (2013). *Census 2013*. Retrieved from archive. stats.govt.nz/Census/2013-census.aspx.

Stump, J. & Dixit, P. (2016). *Critical Terrorism Studies: An Introduction to Research Methods*. London & NY: Routledge.

Trump, Donald Jr. (2019, 4 May). @DonaldJTrumpJr, 1.46 am. Twitter.com.

USDoJ. (2019, 23 July). *Justice Department Reviewing the Practices of Market-Leading Online Platforms*. Retrieved from www.justice.gov/opa/pr/justice-department-reviewing-practices-market-leading-online-platforms.

US Embassy and Consulate in New Zealand. (2019, 15 May). *Statement on Christchurch Call for Action*. Retrieved from web.archive.org/web/20190713 140826/https://nz.usembassy.gov/statement-on-christchurch-call-for-action/.

USFTC. (2019, 24 July). *Statement of Chairman Joe Simons and Commissioners Noah Joshua Phillips and Christine S. Wilson in re Facebook, Inc*. Retrieved from www.ftc.gov/public-statements/2019/07/statement-chairman-joe-simons-commissioners-noah-joshua-phillips-christine.

Walquist, C. (2019, 19 March). Ardern says she will never speak name of Christchurch suspect. *Guardian*. Retrieved from www.theguardian.com/world/2019/mar/19/new-zealand-shooting-ardern-says-she-will-never-speak-suspects-name.

Ward, V. (2019, 20 March). Brenton Tarrant: The 'ordinary white man' turned mass murderer. *Telegraph*. Retrieved from www.telegraph.co.uk/news/0/brenton-tarrant-ordinary-white-man-turned-mass-murderer/.

Wilson, M. (2018, 10 August). The hardest job in Silicon Valley is a living nightmare. *Fast Company*. Retrieved from www.fastcompany.com/90263921/the-hardest-job-in-silicon-valley-is-a-living-nightmare.

Wong, J. (2019, 5 August). 8chan: The far-right website linked to the rise in hate crimes. *Guardian*. Retrieved from www.theguardian.com/technology/2019/aug/04/mass-shootings-el-paso-texas-dayton-ohio-8chan-far-right-website.

YouTube Official Blog. (2019, 24 July). *Global Internet Forum to Counter Terrorism: An Update on Our Progress*. Retrieved from youtube.googleblog.com/search?updated-max=2019-07-31T08:11:00-07:00&max-results=7.

3

Becoming civic actors

Sally Wheeler

Here the Christchurch Call to Action is set in two contexts: the history of the livestreaming of violent events and the argument of technology companies that they are mere relayers of user-generated content. The second of these contexts is parlayed into an argument that technology companies should be seen as having the same responsibilities to the societies they operate in as all other large corporate actors. Despite being expressed at the international level with states as its audience, the response to the Christchurch Call will be, by structural necessity, at the domestic level. The call opens up an opportunity for technology companies to design and embed digital ethics in the societies in which they operate. This chapter closes by examining how this might be achieved.

Live footage of violence

The immediate background to the Christchurch Call of May 2019 was the livestreaming of a mass-shooting event that ended in considerable loss of life. It is worth remembering that the transmission of live footage of events of violence is not a particularly new phenomenon. It is something to which we have been exposed for a number of years and to some extent desensitised. Those of us in our mid-50s and older may well remember the fatal terrorist attack on the Israeli team at the Munich Olympics in early September 1972 that played out on television screens in real time across the northern hemisphere, and the killing of two British Army corporals at a funeral in Northern Ireland, coverage of which interrupted the BBC's Saturday afternoon sports program in March 1988 (Engle, 2018). The distinguishing feature of more recent events is that the second generation of the internet – Web 2.0 – enables user-generated content to be uploaded for global viewing. Livestreaming of terror-related events by unconnected bystanders has become depressingly familiar in recent years. The Brussels Airport and Metro attacks in March 2016 were uploaded live with commentary supplied by social media users in the vicinity. A gun battle between police and a sniper who had already shot five police officers that day in Dallas in July 2016 was relayed live on Facebook. The absence of a newscaster and the presence of a bystander as the link to the event makes it seem psychologically closer, even more so when the perpetrator controls the livestreaming.

In March 2019 the perpetrator of the Christchurch terrorist attack livestreamed his own actions across the world using a Facebook account. Facebook removed the footage of the attack as soon as it was alerted to its presence by the police; however, this was after the attack had ended, meaning that Facebook's content-moderation software had not detected it. Before Facebook's removal of the video, some 4,000 people had viewed it. Subsequently 300,000 versions of it were successfully uploaded and then removed by moderators and a further 1.2 million upload attempts were intercepted by Facebook software and blocked (Whittaker, 2019). While this shielding limited many Facebook users from viewing the event, it was still available on websites such as 4chan and 8chan (now 8kun) until mainstream ISP providers in Australia and Aotearoa New Zealand such as Telstra and Vodafone blocked it (Brennan, 2019; Brodkin, 2019). The Christchurch attack was a racially motivated, white supremacist attack. It has been followed by similarly motivated and executed attacks (each involving the posting of a racist manifesto to an internet forum followed by livestreaming the actual attack) in Poway in the US in April 2019 and in Halle in Germany in October 2019. We might conclude that whatever protocols were put in place regarding the takedown of material following Christchurch have yet to become successful.

Media corporations or technology corporations – does it matter?

The availability of this user-generated content is used to support the argument of social media platforms such as Twitter and Facebook, and digital media corporations such as Google and Apple, that they are not 'media' corporations in the sense that print and broadcast service providers are, but, rather, are technology corporations (Barns, 2020, pp. 35–52) and online service providers (OSPs). They do not produce original content but instead distribute the content made by others, whether those others are, inter alia, individual users, political parties or large corporations. The line between content creation and content distribution is not perhaps as clear as is being suggested; satellite broadcasters such as Sky in many of their operations might be seen as primarily distributors of content produced by others rather than content producers. Like mainstream print and broadcast media, advertising revenue is of huge strategic importance to the business model that OSPs are employing and this shared dependence brings the two much closer together.

This assertion that social media sites and ISPs are technology corporations is broadly supported by US legislation: the Telecommunications Act 1996 s. 230 protects them from liability for the speech of third parties that they host or distribute, as do Articles 12–14 of the foundational legal framework for online services in the EU, the Electronic Commerce Directive 2000. The European Court of Justice has confirmed in a recent decision (Judgment of the Court, 2021) that this directive does indeed set up a safe harbour by creating protection from liability as long as 'neutrality' is maintained; that is to say that conduct by the social media site or ISP is 'merely technical, automatic and passive' (Judgment of the Court, 2010). Once there is actual knowledge of illegal activity that might come from police or other users in relation to violent conduct or from rightsholders in relation to intellectual property rights infringement, then there needs to be a move towards blocking or removing the content in question.

This distinction is also implicitly recognised by the recent digital platforms inquiry in Australia, the Competition and Consumer Commission *Digital Platforms Inquiry* (ACCC, 2019). There it was proposed that certain specified 'digital platforms' were to implement a voluntary code facilitated by the Australian media regulator, the Australian Communications and Media Authority, to govern their relationships with 'media businesses'.

This voluntary code has recently become the subject of an intense disagreement between the Australian Government and Facebook in particular. Being classified as technology rather than media corporations also means that regulatory obligations in relation to content that are imposed on media providers in a variety of nation-state settings such as the requirement, for example, to follow particular guidelines in relation to religious affairs broadcasting (UK), giving adequate time to educational material (US) and ensuring that impartial news content rules (UK) do not apply to them (Napoli and Caplan, 2017).

Of course, pressuring for consideration or classification by the state and commentators as technology corporations rather than media corporations does not mean that there is no legislative or regulatory purview of technology corporations with resulting restrictions or compliance obligations; it simply means that these will not be the same as those applied to media corporations (Moe, 2008) and that there is a lobbying opportunity for technology corporations to shape their regulatory environment. There is an expectation from what might broadly be termed *civil society* that all corporations, whatever their industry classification, undertake voluntary, socially oriented activities that go beyond the obvious enhancement of corporate profits (Carroll, 2016) under the label of corporate social responsibility (CSR). Additionally, civil society expects that corporations will behave ethically and responsibly towards their stakeholders, notwithstanding the rather nebulous definition that the term 'stakeholder' enjoys, even if that means corporations going beyond what is required in a strict regulatory sense (Gunningham et al., 2004). This captures the idea of corporations holding a 'social license to operate'. The difference between CSR and the social license is that corporations choose their CSR interventions but fulfilling their social license requires meeting societal expectations and so involves dialogue with stakeholders around the corporate response to regulation and the corporate decision-making process (Moffat et al., 2016). There is an argument that corporate commitment to demonstrable CSR activities and the maintenance of social license increases inexorably for individual corporations in a position of dominance or where they are so central to the lives of citizens that they might be seen as public utility corporations or essential service providers (Andrejevic, 2013). This increased commitment might be viewed as akin to one of civic responsibility.

The idea that technology corporations occupy a position of dominance and/or operate an essential service, in terms of both their infrastructure and activities, is often adopted by those who advocate that antitrust or competition legislation should be applied to them (Wu, 2018). Indeed, this linkage between monopoly or dominant market power, civic or public responsibility, and competition or antitrust regulation is exactly the position taken by two recent state level inquiries (Flew and Wilding, 2021): the Cairncross Review in the UK (Cairncross, 2019) and the aforementioned Australian Inquiry (ACCC, 2019). The idea of using existing regulatory structures or designing new anti-competitive structures (Lawrence and Laybourn-Langton, 2018) to deal with the perceived monopoly position of technology corporations is one that is well rehearsed from within the disciplines of, inter alia, media studies and law (Thierer, 2013; Ghosh, 2019). There is an assumption made that technology corporations once subjected to antitrust regulation will automatically become civic actors operating in the public interest. However, little consideration is given to what these civic responsibilities might be in the context of technology companies and how they might be arrived at.

The 'ask' of the Christchurch Call

By asserting their identity as technology corporations, reinforced by descriptions of themselves as 'platforms' with stated missions to deliver 'sharing, community and empowerment' (Etlinger, 2019, p. 24), ISPs and social media corporations are ultimately seeking to escape from the idea that they can (or should) exercise editorial control over the content that they host (Gillespie, 2010). The Christchurch Call, at its heart, is a demand that this is exactly what they should do in an open and transparent manner by developing both content screening methodologies and the appropriate technical expertise supported by governments and civil society to filter out material that is supportive of, and advocates for, terrorism and violent extremism. In its three pages of text, the call sets out the paradoxes that surround the internet as a forum for communication. The call is at one and the same time an appeal to protect 'collective security' and recognise the potential impact that the unchecked availability of violent content might have on that, and an assertion that it is possible to do this while respecting and supporting free speech and the role that the internet plays in creating an inclusive and connected society. As a general goal, this is much more difficult to achieve than the call acknowledges.

The events of Christchurch itself apart, the call comes at a difficult juncture for technology companies. Some of those difficulties around the occupation of monopoly positions and liability for distributed content have already been alluded to, but they are really symptomatic of a bigger issue that confronts OSPs: the role of the internet in political life, more generally at the nation-state level, that OSPs facilitate. The internet has gone from being seen as an open public space, an ideal that OSPs have carefully curated through their portrayal of themselves as social libertarians, playing a crucial part in the organisation of protests against authoritarianism and the advance of democracy (Google executive, Wael Ghonim's comment that 'if you want to liberate a society, just give them the internet' comes to mind [Hofheinz, 2011]) to one in which political manipulation through the platforming of fake news in the form of disinformation and the silencing of voices in anti-democratic manner through 'takedown' activities are said to occur (Hoverd et. al, 2021). The longstanding view of OSPs as mere 'relayers' of content has begun to break down, particularly in the EU and in its member states where values such as privacy and respect are seen as at least the equal of the US First Amendment idol of free speech, and are often protected by the criminal law of member states.

The cultural battle around 'cancel culture' is a useful illustration of the general dilemma that OSPs and wider society face. Social media allows a protest movement around a particular institutional activity or person to grow in strength organically thus allowing the resulting collective view to exert, often successfully, pressure for the cancellation of an activity or personal appearance. In this instance the voiceless have been given voice but at the expense of the expression of a perfectly legal view or the conduct of a legitimate activity. In more specific terms, having been lauded as the organising forum for the Arab Spring a decade ago (Clarke and Kocak, 2020), OSPs, particularly Facebook, are now under pressure around a number of alleged misconduct issues: misuse of personal data via Cambridge Analytica during the 2016 US Presidential Election; the manipulation of platform algorithms (aka filter bubbles and echo chambers), to allow the targeting of particular categories of British voters during the Brexit referendum in breach of UK electoral law; and the failure to prevent, through content removal and individual suspensions of users, the organisation of acts of violence by Myanmar military officials against the minority Rohingya people.

This last infraction was compounded by Facebook's subsequent refusal to cooperate in a document production request to support The Gambia's action for genocide against Myanmar in relation to the Rohingya before the International Court of Justice (2020). The Oxford Internet Institute reported that there is evidence of organised campaigns of social media manipulation in 70 countries in 2019; this figure has increased steadily from the institute's first report in 2017 (Bradshaw and Howard, 2019). There is no suggestion that OSPs endorse this manipulation but it does indicate that their 'takedown' policies (or absence thereof) allow it to happen. Both Facebook and Twitter, as platforms, seem to give more latitude to elected officials, or authority figures at least, than to other individuals in terms of when they apply takedown policies (York, 2021). Presumably, their thinking is that those who have been elected have had their perspectives democratically endorsed and that their speech is per se newsworthy (Kang and Isaac, 2019). Given that the utterances and actions of politicians and elected officials will garner more interest within the community, it is to be hoped they are not inciting violence or projecting hate speech. Recent events in the US and parts of Europe would call this assumption into question as we see the rise of violent white nationalism and populist authoritarian political regimes, both of which are thought to be potential triggers for the occurrence of online violent and extremist content (Kaakinen et al., 2018). Even the 'elected official' position can break down; Hezbollah, for example, holds seats in the Lebanese Parliament but is banned from Facebook because in the US, Hezbollah is a designated foreign terror organisation under the Immigration and Nationality Act 1965, s. 219.

The Christchurch Call features several joint undertakings from governments and OSPs to end or at least control the presentation of terrorist-supported content online. There have been other attempts to do this through, for example, the UN Security Council Resolutions (UNHRC, 2018), the EU-supported Internet Forum[1] and technology company-generated initiatives such as Tech Against Terrorism and the Global Internet Forum to Counter Terrorism,[2] but they have concentrated on position-taking, sector by sector, and underwriting their

---

1   See European Internet Forum, www.internetforum.eu/.
2   See Tech Against Terrorism, www.techagainstterrorism.org/about/; Global Internet Forum to Counter Terrorism, gifct.org/. As a result of the Christchurch Call, the GIFCT announced in September 2019 that it would become an NGO, rather than an industry-based body, and would offer a platform for multi-stakeholder engagement.

efforts on what is not necessarily a cooperatively negotiated starting point. What differentiates the Christchurch Call from these previous efforts is the level within both governments and technology companies at which there is engagement, the idea of a partnership approach between not just state and corporate interests but also civil society actors and the clear definition given to its goals (Heldt, 2019). The origin of the Christchurch Call in Aotearoa New Zealand, with the personal investment in it of its prime minister, Jacinda Ardern, is pivotal to creating a new impetus and new space for a familiar discussion. The refusal of the Aotearoa New Zealand administration to use the attacker's name ensured that the focus of media attention remained on the attack itself (Lankford and Tomek, 2018). Aotearoa New Zealand is an unlikely incubator environment for terrorism and all New Zealanders can be seen as victims of this intrusive violence. Aotearoa New Zealand had hitherto not been a state where technology companies were battling against proposed antitrust intervention, privacy legislation and demands to take down fake news and at the same time give protection to free speech rights. This absence of prior history makes the Christchurch Call all the more emotive.

The modalities of this partnership approach commit states to building societal resistance to terrorism and extremism as well as to using regulation in a variety of formats (hard law, soft law, policy tools) to discourage the making and reporting of material and events that support the same. The commitment of OSPs is to transparency of action in general and in particular to the terms of service they operate under in relation to content upload. There is an expectation that those terms of service will be used to achieve a balance between freedom of expression and content removal in the context of the behaviour that the call relates to. In other words, the expectation placed on OSPs for industry-based action is quite a narrow one. The algorithms that drive users with particular activity histories on the internet to violent or extremist content are to be kept under review. In terms of their joint undertakings, there are obligations to civil society around the support of community efforts to counter extremism, obligations to assist smaller internet platforms in developing the capacity to deal with terrorist and extremist content, and obligations to support each other in exchanging information and research that will encourage the development of automatic technical intervention to remove such content (Pandey, 2020).

Answering the Christchurch Call

The Christchurch Call offers three pillars of intervention: the social, the regulatory and the technical. These cannot be seen in isolation from each other. Content moderation is a good example of this interlinking. The call is looking to governments and OSPs to develop content-moderation strategies to combat the uploading of extremist and violent content. This is presented as a technocratic solution to be applied in the event of the failure of the cultural strategies around social inclusion to combat inequality and build resilience to extremist discourses and the regulatory solutions around preventing the production and dissemination of this type of material. Much faith is being placed in technology as an end-game solution to the extent that there are pledges to make algorithmic solutions available across OSPs on the basis of a commercial sharing of innovation. It is possible that in the future machine learning will have evolved sufficiently so that it can do this consistently (Hall et al., 2020) but problems of transparency in what is in many instances the policing of free speech will still occur (Gowra et al., 2020). The events of Christchurch, while not unique, are very much at one end of a long spectrum of potential content-moderation activity.

However, the current reality of content moderation is that it seems to work most efficiently if there is a substantial element of human screening and intervention alongside automated review (Einwiller and Kim, 2020). Human screening or commercial content moderation has its limitations around the quantum and type of material that needs to be viewed. It is a low status, poorly remunerated and stressful job that exposes workers to disturbing words and images (Roberts, 2019). Increasingly, content moderation means the establishment of user-driven moderation tools such as flags, muting ability and the hiding of material (Crawford and Gillespie, 2016). Technology in all its guises reflects its social setting; it is impossible for a technocratic solution not to be embedded in human agency (Katzenbach and Ulbricht, 2019). User-driven content moderation pits user against user without offering any guidance or scaffolding around the appropriate social norms to be applied. There is an increased risk of echo chambers occurring as those not aligned to the position at hand are silenced; some users might find themselves isolated in particular spaces and there might be severe curtailment of free speech opportunities as potential over-censoring takes place by those without a broader view.

The Christchurch Call recognises the presence of an ecosystem between users, content, OSPs and the global reach of their business in the sense that any possible solution requires the sharing of innovation and new expertise. What the call does not explicitly deal with are the problems posed by the fragmented nature of the *tech stack* that underpins internet activity. Six very large technology companies are signatures to the call: Amazon, Facebook, Google, Twitter, YouTube and Microsoft (what we might call the usual suspects), and they are joined by two French companies, Qwant, a search engine, and Dailymotion, a video-sharing platform. Behind these platforms and search engines sit layers of other specialised technical service firms, inter alia, domain name registrars, hosting services, content delivery networks, internet service firms and security firms. Any web presence depends on the seamless interlocking of these services. The firms in the different layers of the *tech stack* will have terms of service around the screening of content, the takedown of content and ultimately a denial of service. Following their own policies places these firms in the position of deciding what material appears on the internet, who can view that material, and, ultimately, what groups are represented and which voices are heard.

The complexity of the *tech stack* allows the creators and purveyors of violent and extremist material to burrow further into the recesses of the internet. We might assume that the largest OSPs, like the ones that signed the Christchurch Call, operate in similar ways and on reasonably similar terms of service. We know comparatively little about how the smaller, single service firms, without which the internet could not function, operate (Gillespie et al., 2020). At times we might be pleasantly surprised; Facebook may have eventually removed the video of the Christchurch attacker and by doing so made it inaccessible to many casual users but it was the action of a small content delivery network firm (Cloudflare) that resulted in the shutdown of more sinister sites dedicated to racist outpourings that were also carrying it (Donovan, 2019). However, as a general principle, to be successful in their aim of preventing the upload of violent, extremist material the signatories to the call are hoping that the engine room of the internet embedded in the *tech stack* endorses and follows their approach.

The Christchurch Call lacks a geographic or regulatory anchor to the nation-state. It is an aspirational document aimed at inter-state cooperation as evidenced by its internal references to 'partner countries', and future inter-governmental meetings such as the G20 and the G7.

This is unsurprising in that the Christchurch Call was assembled on the back of the Paris Call that had been launched by President Macron of France in the days following the centenary of the 1918 armistice. The Paris Call focused on acknowledging the need of individuals for cyber security and how they should be seen essentially as non-combatants in any cyber attacks (the new warfare) launched by rogue governments or hackers and afforded assistance by technology companies and states. The crossover with the Paris Call explains why two French technology companies were signatures to the Christchurch Call. Taken together, these two interventions by national leaders with their appeals to multilateralism across a broad range of stakeholders can be seen as the beginning of *techdiplomacy* (Smith and Browne, 2019, pp. 109–30). The Christchurch Call has called OSPs to account in a very public way and opened up a dialogue space that, from a reputational standpoint, is impossible for them to resist.

However, there is unlikely to be supranational agreements of substance around removing violent and terrorist material from the internet emerging from these sorts of discussions in the short to medium term. Multilateral agreements in any area require extensive negotiation and frequently, even then, require implementation and enforcement, post-interpretation, at the domestic state level. There is no internationally agreed definition of terrorism (Hardy and Williams, 2011). National legal systems have very different definitions of hate speech and no agreement on what is harmful (Nemes, 2002). The possibility of either of these things becoming the subject of international agreement is very low indeed. Civil society as the Christchurch Call uses the term is a reference to the broad polity rather than a suggestion of any structured representative engagement with particular interest groups. Interventions are likely to work rather better if they carry an element of co-design or endorsement from the user sector.

For technology companies, an understanding of each national context in which they operate in terms of their own market position and wider political and cultural norms is essential, as it is that national context that will inform regulatory solutions, the possibilities for self-regulation and civic responsibility, and the potential for amelioration by CSR activities (Thompson, 2019). In terms of a general example of national context, we know that unrestricted free speech as a right has much more support in the US than it does in Germany (Wike, 2016) because each has a very different cultural setting around the exercise of individual rights. In more specific terms, Facebook does not allow postings from the UK group Britain First, which has a right-wing political orientation, because much of their discourse is around the promotion of racial and religious hatred. However, Britain First, no matter how distasteful one finds the positions they advocate for, is not a proscribed organisation in the UK. A denial of platform by the UK's most popular social media site, judged by commercially available statistics (Statista, 2020), risks giving credence to claims of victimisation and differential treatment from their supporters. It pushes these sorts of users into darker, less accessible places on the internet, such as Gab, Parler and Telegram, and towards the business actors that support them (Murphy and Venkataramakrishnan, 2021). It also makes their rhetoric more attractive to some sections of UK society that see themselves as disconnected from the political mainstream.

The Christchurch Call in domestic settings

MGAFA (Microsoft, Google, Apple, Facebook and Amazon) are the world's largest companies by market capitalisation, and all headquartered on the west coast of the US. There are significant differences between them in terms of their business scope (e.g. Amazon has a large physical distribution network and Apple is mainly a hardware business, while Google and Facebook are largely an online presence only) but each dominates in their particular segment: for example, Google in the global search market, Facebook in the digital advertising market, Amazon in the e-commerce market (Barwise and Watkins, 2018). The shift observed around the internet moving from, at worst, a benign intervention creating a new and free public space based on shared values of non-profit making and little state interference to the internet as a purveyor of harmful and dangerous material, a harvester and seller of personal data and a denier of free speech controlled by this small number of globally powerful companies assembling huge profits (a narrative that is not entirely true as demonstrated by the discussion of the *tech stack* but plausible enough to raise concerns [Noam, 2016]), places the activities of these companies under scrutiny in nation-states.

The Christchurch Call secures that national-level scrutiny wonderfully well, as Aotearoa New Zealand, like Australia and much of the rest of the world, does not have a domestic OSP industry. If US-located technology companies can be used to promote a terrible event happening in a place known mostly for rugby union and tourism, then these technology companies can be drawn into the promotion of extremist violence anywhere. This ability to promote and support undesirable activities in individual states across the world must be reined in (Smith, 2018). This negative perception of technology companies (termed *techlash*) at the national level sits alongside popular concerns about the activities of the corporate sector more generally. The retreat of the state under a philosophy of New Public Management in many developed countries has pushed the provision of previously state-led services into the hands of private sector corporations. Access to these services is frequently dictated by technology corporations through devices and digital platforms. Public scrutiny of corporate activities has followed and particular ire has been directed at, inter alia, low taxation revenue raised from non-domiciled corporations with apparently large profits, a description that certainly fits MGAFA when they operate outside the US (Davidson, 2014); rising executive pay in a climate of largely stagnant wage remuneration for rank and file employees; and the need for demonstrably responsible innovation and behaviour to ameliorate harmful activities.

A number of states have embarked upon public inquiries, or their equivalent, into the power and influence of OSPs in recent years, both before and after the Christchurch Call, and how best to achieve effective governance of them on the national stage: India, Aotearoa New Zealand, Germany, France, the UK, Canada, The Netherlands, Switzerland, the US and Australia. Australia's direct response to the events of Christchurch was to pass the *Criminal Code Amendment (Sharing of Abhorrent Violent Material) Act 2019* (Cth) in April 2019, which means, of course, that this legislation was not informed by the Christchurch Call or the discussions around it (Douek, 2020). The 'right to be forgotten' litigation between Spain and Google, as well as explaining the rights of EU citizens in relation to private facts (Rallo, 2018), demonstrates that OSPs can accommodate segmentation of their services on geographic lines and so can tolerate different governance settings in different jurisdictions. The presence of the Christchurch Call, state-based responses to it and national inquiries, both extant and new, have seen OSPs rush to model themselves as responsible self-governing organisations through the adoption of voluntary codes and oversight mechanisms. The Facebook Oversight Board is one such response. It is a body of 40 or so lawyers, academics and commentators drawn from around the world by Facebook. Its remit is to act independently of Facebook, reviewing a sample of the organisation's decisions around content-moderation oversight to see if it complies with its own policy (Klonick, 2020). While it is an interesting venture into the feasibility of crowd-sourcing public opinion in the international arena, it is unlikely to have much practical effect in an area where the feasibility of global governance is severally challenged.

The Facebook Oversight Board is a classic example of self-regulation in that it is an entirely responsive mechanism by the company that attracts much attention but actually requires Facebook to do very little over and above what it already does in the area of content moderation. It has no specific deliverable in terms of stimulating behavioural change. Facebook's shareholders have no need to panic that corporate profits will be impacted by the decision to adopt this strategy. In most jurisdictions, regulation is used to signal the lowest level of performance or conduct that is considered to be consistent with current societal cultural norms and acceptable to the state in terms of the enforcement mechanisms that need to be in place (Bunting, 2018). Domestic jurisdictions recognise that their regulatory enforcement powers do not go beyond their territorial borders and that in both legislative content and enforcement, technological innovation is frequently ahead and will only move further ahead (Hemphill, 2019).

Regulation, particularly the currently fashionable principles-based regulation, is used to stimulate corporate actors to operate over and above it in a way that it is consistent with civic responsibility. This civic responsibility is often 'soft-signalled' by the adoption of a co-designed 'code of ethics'. This is particularly important in the context of OSPs, which are the ultimate societal gatekeeper in terms of the control they have over access to information, communication and services (Metoyer-Duran, 1993). In these circumstances, gatekeepers have a responsibility to support the public interest (Shapiro, 2000). As Taddeo (2019) expresses it:

> [Civic] responsibilities require OSPs to consider the impact of their services … on the societies in which they operate, take into account … ethical benefits and risks, and act so [as] to maximize the former and mitigate the latter. Ethical considerations need to become a constitutive part of their … business model.

Regulatory compliance by OSPs is necessary but on its own it is insufficient to create an environment where OSPs respond continuously and positively at pace with technological developments and in societal interests to create better outcomes (Floridi, 2018). Other industries, for example those in the banking and finance sector in the aftermath of the global financial crisis, have similarly rehabilitated themselves.

The rights set out in the Universal Declaration of Human Rights and the expression they are given in a society is an obvious starting point to determine what values should shape OSP practices in pursuit of civic responsibility. Human rights are obligations of the state but in 2011 the UN adopted the Guiding Principles on Business and Human Rights, which calls on corporations as private actors to respect human rights (UNHRC, 2011). We might think that it is important to protect users' privacy, to correct and prevent biases in information and safeguard the democratic process. Core human rights to be respected would include expression, personal security and dignity, freedom from all forms of discrimination and freedom of exposure to harm and harmful content (Suzor et al., 2018). Transparency of action by OSPs underpins all these values. Accountability and structures for accountability are something that public and quasi public institutions must exhibit. It is within the ambit of these fundamental rights that policies on content moderation should sit. This tie to fundamental rights is an aspirational starting point for a discussion around OSPs and civic responsibility. Few democratic states have a complete articulation of a human rights–compliant framework in their constitutional setting or in supporting legislation. This is true of the US with its grand republican constitution and Germany with its concern for the prevention of hate speech and, in the aftermath of World War II, the protection of the truth (Article 19, 2018). Australia starts from the position of a constitutional settlement, which contains only five limited individual rights and no meaningful domestic discourse about rights or ethics at the nation-state level (Wheeler, 2020).

Constitutional recognition of a particular right is important in assessing its place in society but it is not definitive. Deciding on the values that underpin civic responsibility and how conflicting values should be weighed against each other will be a process of negotiation that involves political actors, civil society and users on a national basis. Users are particularly important contributors to this negotiation as much of OSPs' activity involves interaction with user content. If OSPs think of these fundamental rights at all, it is in a context that is informed by corporate norms (Jørgensen, 2017). We know that these corporate norms are likely to come from a fundamentally libertarian standpoint that draws on the American individualist tradition (van Dijck et al., 2018). The ways in which OSPs organise to construct their civic responsibilities will be dependent on how democratic dialogue operates within individual states. The occurrence of serious events makes society-wide discussions, megalogues in Etzioni's (2002) terms, which span different levels of informal and formal governance more possible. The terrorist attack of March 2019 in Christchurch is one such event.

References

ACCC. (2019). *Digital Platforms Inquiry: Final Report.* Retrieved from www.accc.gov.au/publications/digital-platforms-inquiry-final-report.

Andrejevic, M. (2013). Public service media utilities: Rethinking search engines and social networking as public goods. *Media International Australia*, 146, 123–32. doi.org/10.1177/1329878x1314600116.

Article 19. (2018). *Germany: Responding to 'Hate Speech'.* Retrieved from www.article19.org/wp-content/uploads/2018/07/Germany-Responding-to-%E2%80%98hate-speech%E2%80%99-v3-WEB.pdf.

Barns, S. (2020). *Platform Urbanism.* Singapore: Palgrave Macmillan.

Barwise, P. & Watkins, L. (2018). The evolution of digital dominance. In M. Moore & D. Tambini (Eds). *Digital Dominance* (pp. 21–49). Oxford: Oxford University Press.

Bradshaw, S. & Howard, P. (2019). *The Global Disinformation Disorder: 2019 Global Inventory of Organised Social Media Manipulation*, Project on Computational Propaganda, Oxford. Retrieved from comprop.oii.ox.ac.uk/wp-content/uploads/sites/93/2019/09/CyberTroop-Report19.pdf.

Brennan, D. (2021, 19 March). 4chan, 8chan, LiveLeak and others blocked by Australian internet corporations over mosque massacre video. *Newsweek.* Retrieved from www.newsweek.com/christchurch-attack-video-australia-block-internet-isps-telstra-vodafone-1368174.

Brodkin, J. (2019, 21 March). 4chan, 8chan blocked by Australian and NZ ISPs for hosting shooting video. *Ars Technica.* Retrieved from arstechnica.com/tech-policy/2019/03/australian-and-nz-isps-blocked-dozens-of-sites-that-host-nz-shooting-video/.

Bunting, M. (2018). From editorial obligation to procedural accountability: Policy approaches to online content in the era of information intermediaries. *Journal of Cyber Policy*, 2, 165–86. doi.org/10.1080/23738871.2018.1519030.

Cairncross, F. (2019). *The Cairncross Review: A Sustainable Future for Journalism.* Retrieved from www.gov.uk/government/publications/the-cairncross-review-a-sustainable-future-for-journalism.

Carroll, A. (2016). Carroll's pyramid of CSR: Taking another look. *International Journal of Corporate Social Responsibility.* doi.org/10.1186/s40991-016-0004-6.

Clarke, K. & Kocak, K. (2020). Launching revolution: Social media and the Egyptian uprising's first movers. *British Journal of Political Science*, 50, 1025–45. doi.org/10.1017/s0007123418000194.

Crawford, K. & Gillespie, T. (2016). What is a flag for? Social media reporting tools and the vocabulary of complaint. *New Media and Society*, 18, 410–28. doi.org/10.1177/1461444814543163.

Davidson, S. (2014). *Multinational Corporations, Stateless Income and Tax Havens.* London ACCA. Retrieved from www.accaglobal.com/gb/en/technical-activities/technical-resources-search/2014/march/multinational-corporations-stateless-income-and-tax-havens.html.

Donovan, J. (2019). Navigating the tech stack: When, where and how should we moderate content? In *Models for Platform Governance* (pp. 15–19). Canada: CIGI. Retrieved from www.cigionline.org/articles/navigating-tech-stack-when-where-and-how-should-we-moderate-content/.

Douek, E. (2020). Australia's 'abhorrent violent material' law: Shouting 'nerd harder' and drowning out speech. *Australian Law Journal*, 94, 41–60.

Einwiller, S. & Kim, S. (2020). How online content providers moderate user-generated content to prevent harmful online communication: An analysis of policies and their implementation. *Policy and Internet*, 12, 184–206. doi.org/10.1002/poi3.239.

Engle, V. (2018). *The Funeral Murders.* Retrieved from www.vanessaengle.com/the-funeral-murders.

Etlinger, S. (2019). What's so difficult about social media platform governance? In *Models for Platform Governance* (pp. 20–26). Canada: CIGI. Retrieved from www.cigionline.org/articles/whats-so-difficult-about-social-media-platform-governance/.

Etzioni, A. (2002). The good society. *Seattle Journal for Social Justice*, 1, 83–96.

Flew, T. & Wilding, D. (2021). The turn to regulation in digital communication: The ACCC's digital platforms inquiry and Australian media policy. *Media, Culture and Society*, 43, 48–65. doi.org/10.1177/0163443720926044.

Floridi, L. (2018). Soft ethics and the governance of the digital. *Philosophy and Technology*, 31, 1–8.

Ghosh, D. (2019, 30 May). Don't break up Facebook – treat it like a utility. *Harvard Business Review*. Retrieved from hbr.org/2019/05/dont-break-up-facebook-treat-it-like-a-utility.

Gillespie, T. (2010). The politics of platforms. *New Media and Society*, 12, 347–64.

Gillespie, T., Aufderheide, P., Carmi, E., Gerrard, Y., Gorwa, R., Matamoros-Fernández, A., Roberts, S. T., Sinnreich, A. & Myers West, S. (2020). Expanding the debate about content moderation: Scholarly research agendas for the coming policy debates. *Internet Policy Review*, 9(4), 1–29. doi.org/10.14763/2020.4.1512.

Gowra, R., Binns, R. & Katzenbach, C. (2020). Algorithmic content moderation: Technical and political challenges in the automation of platform governance. *Big Data and Society.* doi.org/10.1177/2053951719897945.

Gunningham, N., Kagan, R. & Thornton, D. (2004). Social license and environmental protection: Why businesses go beyond compliance. *Law and Social Inquiry*, 29, 307–41. doi.org/10.1111/j.1747-4469.2004.tb00338.x.

Hall, M., Logan, M., Ligon, G. & Derrick, D. (2020). Do machines replicate humans? Toward a unified understanding of radicalizing content on the open social web. *Policy and the Internet*, 12, 109–38. doi.org/10.1002/poi3.223.

Hardy, K. & Williams, G. (2011). What is terrorism? Assessing domestic legal definitions. *UCLA Journal of International Law and Foreign Affairs*, 16, 77–162.

Heldt, A. (2019). Let's meet halfway: Sharing new responsibilities in a digital age. *Journal of Information Policy*, 9, 336–69. doi.org/10.5325/jinfopoli.9.2019.0336.

Hemphill, T. (2019). 'Techlash', responsible innovation and the self-regulatory organisation. *Journal of Responsible Innovation*, 6, 240–47. doi.org/10.1080/23299460.2019.1602817.

Hofheinz, A. (2011). Nextopia? Beyond revolution 2.0. *International Journal of Communication* 5, 1417–34. Retrieved from ijoc.org/index.php/ijoc/article/view/1186.

Hoverd, W. Salter, L. & Veale, K. (2021). The Christchurch Call: Insecurity, democracy and digital media – can it really counter online hate and extremism? *SN Social Sciences.* doi.org/10.1007/s43545-020-00008-2.

International Court of Justice. (2020). *Application of the Convention on the Prevention and Punishment of the Crime of Genocide (The Gambia v. Myanmar)*. Retrieved from www.icj-cij.org/public/files/case-related/178/178-20200123-SUM-01-00-EN.pdf.

Jørgensen, R. (2017). What platforms mean when they talk about human tights: Platforms and human rights. *Policy and Internet*, 9, 280–96. doi.org/10.1002/poi3.152.

Judgment of the Court (Grand Chamber). (2010, 23 March). Google France SARL and Google Inc v Louis Vuitton Malletier SA. C-236/08, para 113. Retrieved from curia.europa.eu/juris/liste.jsf?num=C-236/08.

Judgment of the Court (Grand Chamber). (2021, 22 June). YouTube and Cyando. Document 62018CJ0682. Retrieved from eur-lex.europa.eu/legal-content/en/TXT/?uri=CELEX:62018CJ0682.

Kaakinen, M., Oksanen, A. & Räsänen, P. (2018). Did the risk of exposure to online hate increase after the November 2015 Paris attacks? A group relations approach. *Computers in Human Behavior*, 78, 90–97. doi.org/10.1016/j.chb.2017.09.022.

Kang, C. & Isaac, M. (2019, 18 Oct). Defiant Zuckerberg says Facebook won't police political speech. *New York Times*. Retrieved from www.nytimes.com/2019/10/17/business/zuckerberg-facebook-free-speech.html.

Katzenbach, C. & Ulbricht, L., (2019). Algorithmic governance. *Internet Policy Review*, 8, 1–18. doi.org/10.14763/2019.4.1424.

Klonick, K. (2020). The Facebook Oversight Board: Creating an independent institution to adjudicate online free expression. *Yale Law Journal*, 129, 2418–99. Retrieved from www.yalelawjournal.org/feature/the-facebook-oversight-board.

Lankford, A. & Tomek, S. (2018). Mass killings in the United States from 2006 to 2013: Social contagion or random clusters? *Suicide and Life-Threatening Behavior*, 48, 459–67. doi.org/10.1111/sltb.12366.

Lawrence, M. & Laybourn-Langton, L. (2018). *The Digital Commonwealth: From Private Enclosure to Collective Benefit*. IPPR. Retrieved from www.ippr.org/research/publications/the-digital-commonwealth.

Metoyer-Duran, C. (1993). Information gatekeepers. *Annual Review of Information Science and Technology*, 28, 111–50.

Moe, H. (2008). Dissemination and dialogue in the public sphere: A case for public service media online. *Media, Culture and Society*, 30, 319–36. doi.org/10.1177/0163443708088790.

Moffat, K., Lacey, J., Zhang, A. & Leipold, S. (2016). The social licence to operate: A critical review. *Forestry*, 89, 477–88. doi.org/10.1093/forestry/cpv044.

Murphy, H. & Venkataramakrishan, S. (2021, 15 January). Far-right turns to encrypted platforms to stoke further unrest. *Financial Times*. Retrieved from www.ft.com/content/f5c4679b-20c5-4b68-bb6d-958f17385183.

Napoli, P. & Caplan, R. (2017). Why media corporations insist they're not media corporations, why they're wrong, and why it matters. *First Monday*, 22, 5 (May). doi.org/10.5210/fm.v22i5.7051.

Nemes, I. (2002). Regulating hate speech in cyberspace: Issues of desirability and efficacy. *Information and Communications Technology Law*, 11, 193–220. doi.org/10.1080/1360083022000031902.

Noam, E. (2016). From the internet of science to the internet of entertainment. In J. Bauer & M. Latzer (Eds), *Handbook on the Economics of the Internet* (pp. 553–70). Cheltenham: Edward Elgar. doi.org/10.4337/9780857939852.

Pandey, P., (2020). One year since the Christchurch Call to Action: A review. *ORF Issue Brief No. 389*. Retrieved from www.orfonline.org/research/one-year-since-the-christchurch-call-to-action-a-review/.

Rallo, A. (2018). *The Right to be Forgotten on the Internet: Google v Spain*. Washington DC: EPIC.

Roberts, S (2019). *Behind the Screen: Content Moderation in the Shadows of Social Media*. New Haven: Yale Uni Press.

Shapiro, A. (2000). *The Control Revolution: How the Internet is Putting Individuals in Charge and Changing the World We know*. New York: Public Affairs.

Smith, A. (2018, 30 April). Declining majority of online adults say the internet has been good for society. Pew Research Centre. Retrieved from www.pewresearch.org/internet/2018/04/30/declining-majority-of-online-adults-say-the-internet-has-been-good-for-society/.

Smith, B. & Browne, C. (2019). *Tools and Weapons*. New York: Penguin Press.

Statista (2020). *Facebook in the United Kingdom (UK)*. Retrieved from www.statista.com/study/24591/facebook-in-the-united-kingdom-uk-statista-dossier/.

Suzor, N., Van Geelen, T. & Myers West, S. (2018). Evaluating the legitimacy of platform governance: A review of research and a shared research agenda. *International Communication Gazette*, 80, 385–90. doi.org/10.1177/1748 048518757142.

Taddeo, M. (2019). The civic role of online service providers. *Minds and Machines*, 29, 1–7. doi.org/10.1007/s11023-019-09495-6.

Thierer, A. (2013). The perils of classifying social media platforms as public utilities. *CommLaw Conspectus*, 21, 249–97. Retrieved from scholarship.law.edu/commlaw/vol21/iss2/2.

Thompson, P. (2019). Beware of Greeks bearing gifts: Assessing the regulatory response to the Christchurch Call. *The Political Economy of Communication*, 7, 83–104.

UNHRC. (2011). *Guiding Principles on Business and Human Rights: Implementing the United Nations 'Protect, Respect and Remedy' Framework*. A/HRC/17/31. Retrieved from www.ohchr.org/Documents/Publications/GuidingPrinciplesBusinessHR_EN.pdf.

UNHRC. (2018). *Report of the Special Rapporteur on the Promotion and Protection of the Right to Freedom of Opinion and Expression*. A/HRC/38/35. Retrieved from ap.ohchr.org/documents/dpage_e.aspx?si=A/HRC/38/35.

van Dijck, J., Poell, T. & De Waal, M. (2018). *The Platform Society*. New York: OUP.

Wheeler, S. (2020). Human rights. *The Griffith Review*. Retrieved from www.griffithreview.com/articles/human-rights/.

Whittaker, Z. (2019, 18 March). Facebook failed to block 20% of uploaded New Zealand shooter videos. Retrieved from techcrunch.com/2019/03/17/facebook-new-zealand/.

Wike, R. (2016, 12 October). Americans more tolerant of offensive speech than others in the world. Pew Research Center. Retrieved from www.pewresearch.org/fact-tank/2016/10/12/americans-more-tolerant-of-offensive-speech-than-others-in-the-world/.

Wu, T. (2018). *The Curse of Bigness: Antitrust in the New Gilded Age*. New York: Columbia Global Reports. doi.org/10.2307/j.ctv1fx4h9c.

York, J. (2021, 9 January). Users, not tech executives, should decide what constitutes free speech online. *MIT Tech Review*. Retrieved from www.technologyreview.com/2021/01/09/1015977/who-decides-free-speech-online/.

4

Hate the player, not the game: Why did the Christchurch shooter's video look like a game?

Robert Fleet

Loading screen

One of the most remarkable circumstances of the Christchurch shooting incident was the fact that the gunman was able to livestream the first 17 minutes of the attack on the social media platform Facebook. The stream captured the gunman's drive to the Al Noor Mosque until he left the mosque. Perhaps the most notable feature was the use of a first-person perspective achieved with the use of a head camera. For those familiar with video games, first-person perspective is a popular gaming cinematic device. The perspective is most often employed in games that involve guns and shooter-versus-shooter narratives. In effect, the gunman had intentionally replicated the look and feel of a popular mainstream video game genre. Further, the gunman casually referenced a popular internet personality who streams themselves playing games before exiting his vehicle to start the shooting.

The gunman had also concurrently shared a manifesto that supposedly described his motivations and beliefs. However, among the more overtly disturbing material were liberally scattered internet/gaming memes, in-jokes and deliberately provocative, but otherwise nonsensical, text. Once again, the gunman had intentionally tied the shooting back to internet culture and video gaming. Indeed, the manifesto plays on this intersection by sarcastically claiming that violent video games caused the gunman to become the shooter. Many observers suggested that the manifesto was a deliberate joke or distraction perpetrated by the gunman on the public, media and authorities, leading others to question whether the gunman was genuinely motivated by the rhetoric being expressed or whether he was perpetrating a huge internet/gaming cultural joke (Macklin, 2019; Thomas, 2020; Wojtasik, 2020).

This leaves us with a question: why did the gunman go to such lengths to tap into internet and gaming culture? On the one hand, perhaps it *is* a huge internet/gaming cultural joke and the gunman was simply pulling off the biggest troll for fortune and glory in certain dark anonymous places of the internet (a form of intangible internet kudos). On the other hand, the gunman believed in the rhetoric he expressed and was using internet and gaming culture to tap into an audience. The link between the nebulous alt-right rhetoric expressed within video game meta-culture to shock and provoke (for the lulz), and the deadly serious alt-right rhetoric of the so-called true believers is difficult to distinguish. Was this a coincidence and the shooter was simply talking in the language he knew or was this a clever piece of marketing?

We also need to ask ourselves how much assistance the shooter received from the dark places of the internet. The dark places provided both the space and the tools for the shooter to communicate his message to an engaged audience. However, did he work alone or were there voices on the internet making suggestions, providing content, tacitly supporting his actions and anonymously fuelling his beliefs? Without an echo chamber full of conspiracy and disinformation, and in concert with a permissive environment for the promotion of hate, would the actions of the Christchurch shooter have been realised? Was the Christchurch shooter really a lone wolf or was there a pack behind his actions?

This chapter first introduces the myth of the lone, antisocial gamer, and subsequently uncovers the reality of the gaming industry and culture that surrounds it. The chapter then goes on to discuss how the industry and culture of gaming can be divided into the 'good place' and the 'bad place'. Finally, the chapter concludes with a look at the shooter's message, his intended end game and a discussion of what needs attention in the future.

The myth

There is an enduring mythos that surrounds the 'gamer' where the description of the typical gamer is that of the single white male aged in their late teens to early twenties, who is socially awkward and isolated and still lives with his parents or (worse) a single parent, typically a single mother (Zhang and Frederick, 2018). Often used as an epithet, 'gamer' has taken on a negative connotation from early in the cultural understanding of game play that lies outside traditional masculine pursuits of mainstream sports. Gaming was often given the narrative trope of being anti-jock, the opposite of the American high school/college quarterback – homecoming queen dream. This kind of meaning still pervades in many narratives with individuals often quick to distance themselves from the label 'gamer' when observed playing games (Curran, 2011).

This narrative of the anti-jock grew at first from pen-and-paper, dungeons-and-dragons style role-playing games that took place indoors and often took hours or days to play. Within the fantasy setting, players could become the heroes of their own story, wielding mighty powers and conquering fearsome enemies. Of course, with the fantasy setting came accusations of satanic influence. These games, which caused young people to disappear inside for hours and consort with demons, only further tarnished the image of 'gamers' in public perceptions. This would be a recurring issue with the moral outrage over games not disappearing (Martin and Fine, 1991; Waldron, 2005).

There was also a similar narrative in the public consciousness, a narrative of quiet young men who lived alone and kept mostly to themselves. In this narrative the quiet young men are the embodiment of the modern-day bogeyman, the serial killer. However, this narrative contains four pervasive myths about serial killers. It should firstly be noted that serial killers are exceedingly rare in society but remain a popular news media and entertainment topic, which helps to reinforce these myths. The first myth is that all serial killers are men. The second is that all serial killers are Caucasian. The third is that serial killers are isolated, dysfunctional loners. The fourth myth is that serial killers are either mentally ill or evil geniuses (Egger, 2002; Hodgkinson et al., 2017).

The crossover between these narratives is readily apparent. Both narratives draw on the outsider perspective of individuals with a strong focus on the gender and racial (note, not ethnic) aspects as well as the lonely isolated loser–genius. Both narratives describe the gamer and the serial killer as white males who are intelligent but isolated from their peers. There is also, perhaps, an undercurrent of inflated ego and a sense of the world owing them something more, a kind of disregarded entitlement, the longing to be acknowledged as a genius or hero but being unrecognised by others and not being rewarded as such. In total, the 'gamer' narrative weaves together several outsider narratives to construct a single narrative discourse of the mad, bad and sad individual who plays games in isolation from mainstream society: an aberration rather than the norm.

There are claims that there are links between the violence portrayed in video games and the violence that plays out in the physical world. Person versus person (PvP) and person versus environment (PvE) shooter games remain a popular genre of video game (Jansz and Tanis, 2007). The genre remains simple in basic design terms with players being presented with targets (either player-controlled or computer-controlled, sometimes both), which they engage using a variety of weapons including firearms (Hullett and Whitehead, 2010). Claims of a link between violent video games and physical world violence are often brought up by the media when examining the narrative of younger shooters, for example, Columbine (Springhall, 1999). This is not a new phenomenon. It existed in other violent media before video games, for example, John Hinckley Jr (Skoler, 1998). This further feeds into the popular myth linking video games to negative personality traits.

It is easy to see where the Christchurch gunman – an individual with an anti-mainstream identity, withdrawn nature and obsession with the darker places of the internet who has demonstrated the capacity for violence, terror and mass murder (McGowan, 2020) – fits into this mythology. It is also easy to conjure the stereotypical monster described in the gamer/loner/serial killer narrative from the media-derived facts of the case. However, this is perhaps a reductive way of approaching the issue; while it gives some rationality to an irrational act, it ignores the actual reality of gaming, both good and bad.

The reality

The reality of gaming is in stark contrast to this narrative. The modern-day gamer is none of the things described in the previous narrative. For context, as an industry, gaming generated US$152.1 billion revenue in 2019 and is forecast to hit US$196.0 billion by 2022 (Wijman, 2019). In comparison, movies generated a global box office revenue of US$42.5 billion in 2019 (McClintock, 2020). Gaming is big business. A recent report on the Australian gaming industry revealed that nine in 10 households contain at least one gaming device and at least two-thirds of the population play games. Further, 78 per cent of gamers are over the age of 18 with the average age being 34, and 42 per cent of those aged over 65 play. Forty-seven per cent of gamers are female. The average time per day spent playing games is 89 minutes for men and 71 minutes for women (Brand et al., 2019).

This paints a very different picture of what the typical gamer might look like. Gaming is much more widespread and embedded in the daily lives of individuals. With the rise of the personal computer and the internet, games moved from pen-and-paper to the keyboard-and-mouse. Games became increasingly complex and graphically more realistic as computers simultaneously increased in availability and decreased in price (Aarseth, 2013; Paul et al., 2012). The ubiquity of mobile devices and tablets has also led to an increase in access to games. Mobile gaming accounts for nearly half of the revenue generated by the gaming industry (Wijman, 2019). Even though most individuals fall into the category of casual gamers, they are still engaging with games in the same way that more 'hard-core' gamers are; there is simply a difference in scale.

Regarding video game violence and physical world violence, there are still several issues that surround these claims from many quarters. There are studies that link video games with increased aggression (Anderson et al., 2010; Engelhardt et al., 2011; Ferguson, 2007; Ferguson and Kilburn, 2009) though more recent studies call this link into question (Ferguson, 2011; Ferguson et al., 2016; Markey et al., 2015). In short, playing violent video games tends to elevate aggression and confrontational behaviour in the short term; however, this increase is balanced with evidence that cooperative games with violent content can encourage prosocial team building (Greitemeyer and Cox, 2013). The take home is that getting shot at repeatedly tends to make you nervous. Also, for most people the effects are only short term and end relatively quickly once the game play has come to an end.

There is also a definitional issue: it should be noted that the established links are to elevated aggression and not violence. This is an important distinction to make; we can see that all violence is aggression but not all aggression is violent. While this may seem to be arguing semantics, the distinction is important, as there remains no solid evidence linking violence in video games to increased physical world violence. At worst, video games may be seen to elevate the risk of violent responses to provocation rather than be directly linked (Anderson et al., 2010). There is also no clear evidence that the violence in video games desensitises adults to physical world violence (Szycik et al., 2017).

Much of the research focuses on children and adolescent players, which is understandable as this is the group that is perceived to be the most vulnerable and, to an extent, also represents the 'mythical' gamer in people's minds. Within this group, the link to aggression is considered problematic, and there have been steps with ratings and parental controls to limit the exposure of younger gamers to more problematic content (Huesmann, 2007; Hunter Jr et al., 2010; O'Holleran, 2010). In addition, the research indicates that there is more at play than perhaps simply exposure to violence (Ferguson and Olson, 2014). There is ongoing uncertainty about the role that video games play when accounting for the entire set of circumstances and social milieu of the individual. Underlying psychological predispositions to violence may be elevated by video games in both youths and adults, though this is perhaps a side effect of the anxiety and aggressive affect induced in the short term by the game genre (Gentile et al., 2014; Hasan et al., 2012).

While for the normal adult the link between video game violence and physical world violence is not readily apparent, it does exist for small sections of the population who have an underlying predisposition towards violence. The real question is, which comes first, the video game or the predisposition? It would be logical to understand a person with some predisposition towards violence accessing games that are violent as this would allow them to indulge in such violence (Anderson et al., 2010). In a similar way that an ice hockey fan would be attracted to playing an ice hockey simulation, a person with an attraction to shooting may choose to play a game that involves shooting. So, in this way, the myth of the violent serial killing 'gamer' is a somewhat of a self-fulfilling prophecy: those individuals with a predisposition towards violence will naturally be attracted to violent video games. Whether video games contribute to negative outcomes or promote 'gamer' deviance is unclear.

Additionally, there is a growing meta-culture surrounding games that incorporates discussion of in-game, in-character cultures and out-of-game, out-of-character cultures concerned with how to play the game (meta-gaming). By extension, this meta-culture further incorporates other aspects of players' interests, for example, manga (Japanese graphic novels), anime (Japanese animation) and pop cultural references to television, movies and media (Boluk and LeMieux, 2017). Collectively, this meta-culture has strong positive and negative impacts on the way in which the discourse used surrounding games and gaming meta-culture is constructed and used, effectively dividing what would be recognised as gaming into the 'good place' and the 'bad place'.

The good place

Far from the isolated loner, the average gamer is socially connected and an active participant in the culture that surrounds games. In the same report on the Australian gaming industry, it is noted that 66 per cent of players will read or watch a walkthrough of gameplay shared by another player. Forty-one per cent of players watch eSports events, 31 per cent attend eSports events in-person and 38 per cent enjoy the culture that surrounds eSports. Parents who play with their children do so to spend time with their children and as part of inclusive family fun. Fifty-nine per cent of players will play with children in the same room while 25 per cent will play with their partner online. Twenty-seven per cent of players will post gameplay videos of themselves playing a game and 28 per cent participate in cosplay, publicly dressing as fictional characters from games (Brand et al., 2019).

Video games have been linked to pain management and improvements in life satisfaction (Griffiths, 2005; McGuire, 1984; Wang et al., 2008). Video games also have their place in education, with games promoting general knowledge, increasing student creativity and engagement, as well as providing opportunities from vocational and professional training. Video games can promote team building and cooperation as well as strategic thinking to overcome challenges. Video games also have the potential to offer insight into social issues such as epidemiology (Lofgren and Fefferman, 2007), financial market behaviour (Kieger, 2010) and criminal behaviours (Fleet and Nurmikko-Fuller, 2019). The potential for gaming to have a significant impact for good exists.

There is an increasing number of new media celebrities that almost exclusively engage with the public either through directly playing video games or by more indirectly engaging with video game meta-culture. Videos of players playing games have become a popular genre on services such as YouTube and, more recently, dedicated game steaming services such as Twitch (Johnson and Woodcock, 2019). Sponsors are willing to invest significantly in content streamers who may use and endorse products and services to an engaged audience. Often these streamers also move outside of simply playing games to comment on issues to do with modifying games (modding), gaming hardware and other player/streamers in search of content (Lessel et al., 2017). There is also a subgenre (though this terminology is problematic for reasons that will be touched on later) concerning the role that female gamers play in the streaming landscape. So-called 'gamer girls' or 'eGirls' can stream themselves playing games, discussing games and partaking in cosplay for a mostly male audience for which they accept donations, gifts or payments. However, this does not mean that all female gamers/streamers are reduced to this role (Harrison et al., 2016; Ruberg et al., 2019). In parallel to the media celebrity, the celebrity of eSports stars has risen, in some cases to a higher profile than some more mainstream sports. Amid rising public interest, increases in prize money, more widespread sponsorship and the sale of broadcast rights, gamers have taken on the role of professional athletes (Hamari and Sjöblom, 2017).

The ability to generate income from game play and game culture has demonstrated a new legitimacy and regard for games and gamers in general, which in turn has begun to break down some of the stigma and moral panic about the role that games play in everyday society. Game play and game culture are beginning to be incorporated in popular culture in the same way that movies and television shows of the past moved into the zeitgeist of previous eras.

The bad place

With the growth in popularity and familiarity with games and gaming culture, both the good and bad side of game culture has been highlighted. There are larger social and structural issues within gaming that continue to be made apparent as gaming shifts from a pastime to a major mainstream industry and source of income. To illustrate, continuing from the myth that games are a boys-only club, there are strong gender divisions within the industry itself and gamer culture (Assunção, 2016). Games have been predominately developed and marketed to masculine identities, causing much of the game design aesthetics and marketing design to be primarily for the male gaze (Lynch et al., 2016). Male characters, both non-player characters and player-controlled characters (avatars), occupy positions of power and authority. For the player, the male, blank canvas avatar presented by the game often represents ideal masculinities onto which the player can project themselves as the hero/villain of their own fantasy (Trepte et al., 2009). Female characters are often placed in subservient roles to main male protagonist characters; even supposedly strong female characters are often still seen to defer to male characters or be forced into traditional female roles. When a female protagonist is allowed, appearances between male avatars and female avatars are more often strongly divided. Where male avatar's clothing and armour is full-covering and functional, female armours are more often the equivalent of a stainless steel bikini, being revealing and mostly impractical (Hoffswell, 2011; Lynch et al., 2016). This demonstrates how the male gaze affects the basic design principles of games.

This divide is also reflected in the game development industry. From early on, game development was dominated by male identities at the helms of game development studios. This was often the result of computer engineering and computer programming growing out of the STEM disciplines, again a traditionally male dominated and male protected space. This set the scene for a male gaze–oriented gaming design, development and marketing landscape. A common feature of game development exhibitions was the 'booth babe': an attractive young woman employed to stand at industry displays to entice the predominantly male audience to engage with the products being marketed (Cornfeld, 2018; Taylor et al., 2009). What developed was a toxic, hegemonic masculinity that was characterised by white, well-educated men in positions of power (Dunlop, 2007; Fron et al., 2007). The hegemony actively attacks female challengers to the status quo, as seen recently with the 'Gamergate' controversy and the continued and increasingly more frequent revelations of historic sexual and psychological abuse of female gamers and industry workers (Consalvo, 2012; Mortensen, 2018; Salter, 2018).

Female players are often placed in a no-win situation on the revelation that they are, in fact, female. Skilled female players are often challenged to prove that they are not cheating when displaying similar skill levels to male players. In fact, skilled female players are met with open hostility by less skilled male players who feel threatened and 'do not want to get beaten by a girl' or be seen 'to be playing like a girl' by their male peers. Less skilled female players often must suffer the attentions of skilled male players who are likely to instruct them on how to improve – at best an exercise in paternalism, at worst 'mansplaining'. Male players will often 'white knight' (male hero to the rescue) female players to appear sympathetic and well meaning but turn hostile when the level of gratitude is below what was expected (McLean and Griffiths, 2019; Tang et al., 2020). Either way, female players are either reviled or disempowered.

For female streamers there are also some double standards at play. While the work that they perform or the role that they play during that performance is unproblematic, in the same way that we can regard sex work as unproblematic, there is some debate over the ethics of charging money to access this work. Male subscribers and viewers donate gifts and money to the streamer to access content that ranges from public online engagement through to private online engagement, right up to the sharing of 'lewd' content. Again, this is not dissimilar to the range of work provided by sex workers. However, there are two perceived issues: the first that this is virtual engagement – no actual physical engagement is undertaken – yet money and gifts change hands. The second is that there are a significant number of male customers who regard the engagement as exclusive to themselves, or at least engage in that delusion, and who can be quite reactionary once that illusion of intimacy and individual attention is broken. On the one hand, the male subscriber expects a 'girlfriend experience' from the streamer, but on the other hand is offended that the female streamer is not conforming to the idealised version of the 'gamer girl' or 'eGirl' that they hold in their mind (Ruberg et al., 2019). Once again there is a male gaze perspective to the boundaries that are set on the way in which females should be perceived and behave (Cullen and Ruberg, 2019).

These divisions are also played out over race, sexuality and gender issues. Many of the features of so-called 'trash talk' use provocative language centred on insults towards opposition players and vilify people of different racial, gender and/or sexual orientation groups (Leonard, 2004). These attacks can increase once the player is found to be part of one of these groups. While these insults might be seen to be innocuous or part of the accepted gameplay meta-cultural narrative, semi-deliberate, often ignorant, casual attacks still hold weight for the recipient (Fox and Tang, 2017; Tang and Fox, 2016; Wright et al., 2002). More insidious are the players who use this veil of acceptability to disguise outright hate speech and personally hold extremist beliefs (Daniels and LaLone, 2012): a kind of 'don't hate the player, hate the game' defence against bigotry.

Therefore, a common theme of bad gaming culture is one of white male hegemony to the exclusion of females, people of colour and non-heterosexuals. It is also self-reinforcing, with the casual acceptability of racist and sexist speech normalising these attitudes as acceptable and part of gaming culture. This acceptance has caused pockets of gaming culture to strongly overlap with other white, male, racist and sexist subcultures (Daniels and LaLone, 2012; Leonard, 2004) – subcultures that thrive on the sharing and posting of hatred, ideology and conspiracy (Lauterbach, 2009). Race and gender boundaries are placed on the expected roles and behaviours of the members of the gaming culture who do not conform to the standards imposed by the hegemony, and there can be a firm reaction from the hegemony when these role expectations and boundaries are crossed.

An intersection exists between these marginal, normalised, casually racist, sexist and reactionary spaces and the alt-right (far right) and incel (involuntary celibates) extremes. Alt-right beliefs centred on the occupation of supposedly white space by non-white individuals and the idea of a conspiracy to eventually replace pure white peoples with mixed race and foreign peoples (the so-called Great Replacement conspiracy) are closely aligned with the perspectives of a minority of gamers. These gamers see games becoming so inclusive and politically correct that, over time, they are eroding the primary gaming theme of the all-white, all-patriotic, all-conquering masculine superhero so that the gamer identity constructed on this ideal is being marginalised. These kinds of appeals to the pure-blooded, patriotic superhero lie at the heart of the identity propaganda associated with the archetypal, national, socialist and fascist movements in the past and into the present (Colley and Moore, 2020; DeCook, 2018).

Incel identities present a similar rhetoric, only rather than being based on race, the ideology is based on gender. The incel community believes in a conspiracy that promotes the belief that collectively, the female population is excluding certain males from access to sex due to various reasons, rendering them involuntarily celibate. Incels tend to blame externalities for their lack of attraction to the female population rather than any of their own shortcomings. In fact, incels usually perceive themselves as quite charming and, in many cases, the ultimate gentlemen.

Incels often tend to view other men who are having sex as graceless brutes who treat females poorly (yet they also think woman want this) or as somehow beating the system and tricking otherwise receptive females into sex to the exclusion of the incel who is 'playing by the rules'. The rhetoric of female selectivity plays into themes found in the Great Replacement conspiracy and racial purity as well as into misguided notions of masculinity and femininity, with men being seen as chivalrous heroes and woman as damsels in distress who pay for being rescued with physical intimacy and devotion (O'Malley et al., 2020; Waśniewska, 2020).

The message

The message that the Christchurch shooter was trying to send was one of racial purity and a new world order that placed white men at the top and relegated others to the status of subhuman subservient slaves – a population of non-white people who knew their place and who lived and worked where they were told. It harked back to propaganda used by fascist regimes: a homeland for all races, ultimately leading to a final solution for the non-white problems. While not explicit, the implication was that women would take on the role of repopulating the pure white races as their duty to white men, women who owed their lives and security from savage other races to white masculine heroes, women who repaid this heroic service with devotion and reproduction.

The aim of sending this message was to awaken the sleeping members of white society to the reality unfolding before their eyes, especially those were deceived into disbelieving or ignoring reality. It was a rallying cry to those members who shared similar ideals but were too afraid to act on them. It was a simple, clear message to the non-white subhumans that their time was up, that honest white men would no longer sit idly by while they were marginalised and bred out of existence. It was a message of hate, intolerance and ignorance. A common style of extremist messaging, it centred on the grand act to draw attention to a perceived issue that would serve as a signal for like-minded people to act and to awaken those who have been deceived (Campion, 2019; Kaati et al., 2016). Similar messages had been played out before, such as in 2011 in Norway, to draw attention to a terrorist's manifesto (Berntzen and Sandberg, 2014), or the Oklahoma bombing in 1995, which was intended to spark a revolution (Michel and Herbeck, 2015). It was an old message delivered via much newer packaging.

The end game

The Christchurch shooter took advantage of the space opened up by the intersection of the casual everyday racist and sexist dialogue used by sectors of the gaming community to provoke and intimidate, and the undercurrent of extremism that feeds on the edges of these casual spaces. It is an easy step to take from casual racist and sexist beliefs into full-blown bigotry. The shooter framed his message using common language from the bad place to both communicate with the extremist audience and to potentially influence those individuals who may already be flirting with extremism. This common language is often poorly controlled by gaming companies and facilitated by anonymous free-for-all internet boards (e.g. 4chan, 8chan). While the people on these fringes see no harm in their jokes and provocations, it allows the space for other stronger rhetoric to hide in plain sight.

The shooter used the language to which he had been socialised to frame his message, a social discourse that is familiar to individuals who sit at the intersection between gaming culture and alt-right extremism. The major debate is whether the shooter simply spoke to his peers in the language to which he was accustomed or whether this was a deliberate and crafted attempt to utilise the social discourse and platform of gaming to reach newer, more sympathetic audiences. Either way, the objective was to provoke a response in the audience. The message could be seen as an extension of the bad place's attitudes and casual bigotry, where the borders are pushed for laughs and point scoring. Conversely, it could be seen as cynically using the space created by the casual bigotry to widen the reach of the extremist views being promulgated.

The final boss

It would be easy to mythologise the shooter based on the existing myth that surrounds gaming and gaming culture. The shooter fits into so many of the categories expressed in the negative stereotype of the lonely, violent gamer. However, the reality is that gaming is much more widespread and social than the stereotype suggests. Gaming is big business and brings with it several social and economic benefits as well as the potential to answer much larger societal questions. Notwithstanding these benefits, there is a permissive element in gaming culture that allows for the normalisation and spread of hate and ignorance. This is where the Christchurch shooter found the platform on which to spread his manifesto. Gaming and internet culture are far from the myth of isolated individuals; rather, they are a networked collective of overlapping and interconnecting spaces that allow individuals to transmit both positive and negative social goods. The edges of this network contain extremist elements that can diffuse into the more casual spaces that have become permissive of bigotry under the guise of just jokes, provocations and slights used to attack those who sit outside the expected norm, which, while not personally representative of those replicating the extremist language, nonetheless serves to normalise it such that it becomes simple for actual extremist beliefs to stealthily continue to exist.

If that is the case and the shooter, rather than being a lone individual who took extreme action, is part of a wider network that reaches both extremist audiences and casual audiences of younger, more easily influenced individuals, we need to take a further look at whether the shooter got help in formulating what could be a rather clever piece of marketing. We also need to look at the gaming industry and gaming culture itself to help improve control of the margins that the extremist groups seem to take advantage of. A more concerted effort to rein in the normalisation of racist and sexist attitudes towards outsiders, both within the industry and within the player base, remains a priority. While steps have been taken recently to improve the representation of minorities in games, and in the people who make games, there seems to be some distance still to travel.

References

Aarseth, E. (2013). Game history: A special issue. *Game Studies,* 13(2). Retrieved from gamestudies.org/1302/articles/eaarseth.

Anderson, C. A., Shibuya, A., Ihori, N., Swing, E. L., Bushman, B. J., Sakamoto, A., Rothstein, H. & Saleem, M. (2010). Violent video game effects on aggression, empathy, and prosocial behavior in Eastern and Western countries: A meta-analytic review. *Psychological Bulletin,* 136(2), 151–73. doi.org/10.1037/a0018251.

Assunção, C. (2016). 'No girls on the internet': The experience of female gamers in the masculine space of violent gaming. *Press Start,* 3(1), 46–65. Retrieved from doaj.org/article/c4d482d0eec74a3b8b3ae3240c75cc23.

Berntzen, L. E. & Sandberg, S. (2014). The collective nature of lone wolf terrorism: Anders Behring Breivik and the anti-Islamic social movement. *Terrorism and Political Violence,* 26(5), 759–779. doi.org/10.1080/0954655 3.2013.767245.

Boluk, S. & LeMieux, P. (2017). *Metagaming: Playing, Competing, Spectating, Cheating, Trading, Making, and Breaking Videogames* (Electronic Mediations 53). University of Minnesota Press. doi.org/10.5749/9781452958354.

Brand, J. E., Jervis, J., Huggins, P. M. & Wilson, T. W. (2019). *Digital Australia 2020: The Power of Games.* Eveleigh, NSW: IGEA. Retrieved from igea.net/2019/07/digital-australia-2020-da20/.

Campion, K. (2019). Australian right wing extremist ideology: Exploring narratives of nostalgia and nemesis. *Journal of Policing, Intelligence and Counter Terrorism,* 14(3), 208–26. doi.org/10.1080/18335330.2019.1667013.

Colley, T. & Moore, M. (2020). The challenges of studying 4chan and the alt-right: 'Come on in the water's fine'. *New Media & Society.* doi.org/10.1177/1461444820948803.

Consalvo, M. (2012). Confronting toxic gamer culture: A challenge for feminist game studies scholars. *Ada: A Journal of Gender, New Media, and Technology,* 1(1), 1–6. dx.doi.org/10.7264/N33X84KH.

Cornfeld, L. (2018). Babes in tech land: Expo labor as capitalist technology's erotic body. *Feminist Media Studies,* 18(2), 205–20. doi.org/10.1080/14680 777.2017.1298146.

Cullen, A. L. & Ruberg, B. (2019). Necklines and 'naughty bits': Constructing and regulating bodies in live streaming community guidelines. In *The Proceedings of the 14th International Conference on the Foundations of Digital Games.* New York: Association for Computing Machinery. doi. org/10.1145/3337722.3337754.

Curran, N. (2011). Stereotypes and individual differences in role-playing games. *International Journal of Role-Playing,* 2, 44–58. Retrieved from ijrp.subcultures.nl/?page_id=226.

Daniels, J. & LaLone, N. (2012). Racism in video gaming: Connecting extremist and mainstream expressions of white supremacy. In D. G. Embrick, J. Tallmadge Wright & A, Lukscas (Eds). *Social Exclusion, Power, and Video Game Play: New Research in Digital Media and Technology* (pp. 85–100). Plymouth, UK: Lexington Books.

DeCook, J. R. (2018). Memes and symbolic violence: #proudboys and the use of memes for propaganda and the construction of collective identity. *Learning, Media and Technology*, 43(4), 485–504. doi.org/10.1080/17439884.2018.1544149.

Dunlop, J. C. (2007). The US video game industry: Analyzing representation of gender and race. *International Journal of Technology and Human Interaction (IJTHI)*, 3(2), 96–109. doi.org/10.4018/jthi.2007040106.

Egger, S. A. (2002). *The Killers Among Us*. New York: Prentice Hall.

Engelhardt, C. R., Bartholow, B. D., Kerr, G. T. & Bushman, B. J. (2011). This is your brain on violent video games: Neural desensitization to violence predicts increased aggression following violent video game exposure. *Journal of Experimental Social Psychology*, 47(5), 1033–36. doi.org/10.1016/j.jesp.2011.03.027.

Ferguson, C. J. (2007). The good, the bad and the ugly: A meta-analytic review of positive and negative effects of violent video games. *Psychiatric Quarterly*, 78(4), 309–16. doi.org/10.1007/s11126-007-9056-9.

Ferguson, C. J. (2011). Video games and youth violence: A prospective analysis in adolescents. *Journal of Youth and Adolescence*, 40(4), 377–391. doi.org/10.1007/s10964-010-9610-x.

Ferguson, C. J. & Kilburn, J. (2009). The public health risks of media violence: A meta-analytic review. *Journal of Pediatrics*, 154(5), 759–63. doi.org/10.1016/j.jpEds2008.11.033.

Ferguson, C. J. & Olson, C. K. (2014). Video game violence use among 'vulnerable' populations: The impact of violent games on delinquency and bullying among children with clinically elevated depression or attention deficit symptoms. *Journal of Youth and Adolescence*, 43(1), 127–36. doi.org/10.1007/s10964-013-9986-5.

Ferguson, C. J., Trigani, B., Pilato, S., Miller, S., Foley, K. & Barr, H. (2016). Violent video games don't increase hostility in teens, but they do stress girls out. *Psychiatric Quarterly*, 87(1), 49–56. doi.org/10.1007/s11126-015-9361-7.

Fleet, R. & Nurmikko-Fuller, T. (2019). The potential for serious spaceships to make a serious difference. In *The Proceedings of the 10th ACM Conference on Web Science*. New York: Association for Computing Machinery. doi.org/10.1145/3292522.3326017.

Fox, J. & Tang, W. Y. (2017). Women's experiences with general and sexual harassment in online video games: Rumination, organizational responsiveness, withdrawal, and coping strategies. *New Media & Society*, 19(8), 1290–307. doi.org/10.1177/1461444816635778.

Fron, J., Fullerton, T., Morie, J. F. & Pearce, C. (2007). *The Hegemony of Play.* Paper presented at the 2007 DiGRA International Conference: Situated Play, University of Tokyo, September 2007. Retrieved from www.digra.org/digital-library/publications/the-hegemony-of-play/.

Gentile, D. A., Li, D., Khoo, A., Prot, S. & Anderson, C. A. (2014). Mediators and moderators of long-term effects of violent video games on aggressive behavior: Practice, thinking, and action. *JAMA Pediatrics*, 168(5), 450–57. doi.org/10.1001/jamapediatrics.2014.63.

Greitemeyer, T. & Cox, C. (2013). There's no 'I' in team: Effects of cooperative video games on cooperative behavior. *European Journal of Social Psychology*, 43(3), 224–28. doi.org/10.1002/ejsp.1940.

Griffiths, M. (2005). Video games and health. *British Medical Journal*, 331. dx.doi.org/10.1136%2Fbmj.331.7509.122.

Hamari, J. & Sjöblom, M. (2017). What is eSports and why do people watch it? *Internet Research*. doi.org/10.1108/intr-04-2016-0085.

Harrison, R. L., Drenten, J. & Pendarvis, N. (2016). Gamer girls: Navigating a subculture of gender inequality. *Consumer Culture Theory*. doi.org/10.1108/s0885-211120160000018004.

Hasan, Y., Bègue, L. & Bushman, B. J. (2012). Viewing the world through 'blood-red tinted glasses': The hostile expectation bias mediates the link between violent video game exposure and aggression. *Journal of Experimental Social Psychology*, 48(4), 953–56. doi.org/10.1016/j.jesp.2011.12.019.

Hodgkinson, S., Prins, H. & Stuart-Bennett, J. (2017). Monsters, madmen … and myths: A critical review of the serial killing literature. *Aggression and Violent Behavior*, 34, 282–89. doi.org/10.1016/j.avb.2016.11.006.

Hoffswell, J. M. (2011). *Female Video Game Characters and the Male Gaze* [Unpublished doctoral dissertation]. Northern Illinois University.

Huesmann, L. R. (2007). The impact of electronic media violence: Scientific theory and research. *Journal of Adolescent Health*, 41(6), S6–S13. doi.org/10.1016/j.jadohealth.2007.09.005.

Hullett, K. & Whitehead, J. (2010). Design patterns in FPS levels. In *The Proceedings of the Fifth International Conference on the Foundations of Digital Games*. New York: Association for Computing Machinery. doi.org/10.1145/1822348.1822359.

Hunter Jr, R. J., Lozada, H. R. & Mayo, A. (2010). Censorship in the video game industry: Government intervention or parental controls. *University of Denver Sports & Entertainment Law Journal*, 9, 54. Retrieved from www.law.du.edu/sports-and-entertainment-law-journal/past-issues.

Jansz, J. & Tanis, M. (2007). Appeal of playing online first person shooter games. *CyberPsychology & Behavior*, 10(1), 133–36. doi.org/10.1089/cpb.2006.9981.

Johnson, M. R. & Woodcock, J. (2019). 'It's like the gold rush': The lives and careers of professional video game streamers on Twitch.tv. *Information, Communication & Society*, 22(3), 336–51. doi.org/10.1080/1369118x.2017.1386229.

Kaati, L., Shrestha, A. & Cohen, K. (2016). *Linguistic Analysis of Lone Offender Manifestos*. Paper presented at the 2016 IEEE international conference on cybercrime and computer forensic (ICCCF). doi.org/10.1109/icccf.2016.7740427.

Kieger, S. (2010). An exploration of entrepreneurship in massively multiplayer online role-playing games: Second Life and Entropia Eniverse. *Journal For Virtual Worlds Research*, 2(4). doi.org/10.4101/jvwr.v2i4.643.

Lauterbach, M. (2009). *Hate Online: Exploring the World of Extremist Internet Culture*. The George Washington University, Ann Arbor.

Leonard, D. (2004). High tech blackface: Race, sports, video games and becoming the other. *Intelligent Agent*, 4(4). Retrieved from www.intelligentagent.com/archive/Vol4_No4_gaming_leonard.htm.

Lessel, P., Vielhauer, A. & Krüger, A. (2017). Expanding video game live-streams with enhanced communication channels: A case study. In *The Proceedings of the 2017 CHI Conference on Human Factors in Computing Systems*. New York: Association for Computing Machinery. doi.org/10.1145/3025453.3025708.

Lofgren, E. T. & Fefferman, N. H. (2007). The untapped potential of virtual game worlds to shed light on real world epidemics. *The Lancet Infectious Diseases*, 7(9), 625–29. doi.org/10.1016/s1473-3099(07)70212-8.

Lynch, T., Tompkins, J. E., van Driel, I. I. & Fritz, N. (2016). Sexy, strong, and secondary: A content analysis of female characters in video games across 31 years. *Journal of Communication*, 66(4), 564–84. doi.org/10.1111/jcom.12237.

Macklin, G. (2019). The Christchurch attacks: Livestream terror in the viral video age. *CTC Sentinel*, 12(6).

Markey, P. M., Markey, C. N. & French, J. E. (2015). Violent video games and real-world violence: Rhetoric versus data. *Psychology of Popular Media Culture*, 4(4), 277–95. doi.org/10.1037/ppm0000030.

Martin, D. & Fine, G. A. (1991). Satanic cults, satanic play: Is 'Dungeons & Dragons' a breeding ground for the devil? *The Satanism Scare*, 107–23. doi.org/10.4324/9781315134741-7.

McClintock, P. (2020). 2019 Global box office revenue hit record $42.5b despite 4 percent dip in US. *Billboard*. Retrieved from www.billboard.com/articles/news/8547827/2019-global-box-office-revenue-hit-record-425b-despite-4-percent-dip-in-us.

McGowan, M. (2020). As the Christchurch shooter faces sentencing, what has Australia learned about far-right terror? *Guardian*. Retrieved from www.theguardian.com/world/2020/aug/23/as-the-christchurch-shooter-faces-sentencing-what-has-australia-learned-about-far-right-terror.

McGuire, F. A. (1984). Improving the quality of life for residents of long term care facilities through video games. *Activities, Adaptation & Aging*, 6(1), 1–7. doi.org/10.1300/j016v06n01_01.

McLean, L. & Griffiths, M. D. (2019). Female gamers' experience of online harassment and social support in online gaming: A qualitative study. *International Journal of Mental Health and Addiction*, 17(4), 970–94. doi.org/10.1007/s11469-018-9962-0.

Michel, L. & Herbeck, D. (2015). *American Terrorist: Timothy McVeigh and the Oklahoma City Bombing*. BookBaby.

Mortensen, T. E. (2018). Anger, fear, and games: The long event of #GamerGate. *Games and Culture*, 13(8), 787–806. doi.org/10.1177/1555412016640408.

O'Holleran, J. (2010). Blood code: The history and future of video game censorship. *Journal on Telecommunication & High Technology. Law*, 8(2), 571–612.

O'Malley, R. L., Holt, K. & Holt, T. J. (2020). An exploration of the involuntary celibate (Incel) subculture online. *Journal of Interpersonal Violence*, September. doi.org/10.1177/0886260520959625.

Paul, P. S., Goon, S. & Bhattacharya, A. (2012). History and comparative study of modern game engines. *International Journal of Advanced Computed and Mathematical Sciences*, 3(2), 245–49.

Ruberg, B., Cullen, A. L. & Brewster, K. (2019). Nothing but a 'titty streamer': Legitimacy, labor, and the debate over women's breasts in video game live streaming. *Critical Studies in Media Communication*, 36(5), 466–81. doi.org/10.1080/15295036.2019.1658886.

Salter, M. (2018). From geek masculinity to Gamergate: The technological rationality of online abuse. *Crime, Media, Culture*, 14(2), 247–64. doi.org/10.1177/1741659017690893.

Skoler, G. (1998). The archetypes and psychodynamics of stalking. In *The Psychology of Stalking* (pp. 85–112). Elsevier. doi.org/10.1016/b978-012490560-3/50024-4.

Springhall, J. (1999). Violent media, guns and moral panics: The Columbine High School massacre, 20 April 1999. *Paedagogica Historica*, 35(3), 621–41. doi.org/10.1080/0030923990350304.

Szycik, G. R., Mohammadi, B., Hake, M., Kneer, J., Samii, A., Münte, T. F. & Te Wildt, B. T. (2017). Excessive users of violent video games do not show emotional desensitization: An fMRI study. *Brain Imaging and Behavior*, 11(3), 736–43. doi.org/10.1007/s11682-016-9549-y.

Tang, W. Y. & Fox, J. (2016). Men's harassment behavior in online video games: Personality traits and game factors. *Aggressive Behavior*, 42(6), 513–21. doi.org/10.1002/ab.21646.

Tang, W. Y., Reer, F. & Quandt, T. (2020). Investigating sexual harassment in online video games: How personality and context factors are related to toxic sexual behaviors against fellow players. *Aggressive Behavior*, 46(1), 127–35. doi.org/10.1002/ab.21873.

Taylor, N., Jenson, J. & De Castell, S. (2009). Cheerleaders/booth babes/*Halo* hoes: Pro-gaming, gender and jobs for the boys. *Digital Creativity*, 20(4), 239–52. doi.org/10.1080/14626260903290323.

Thomas, E. (2020). *Manifestos, Memetic Mobilisation and the Chan Boards in the Christchurch Shooting*. Retrieved from www.jstor.org/stable/resrep25133.7.

Trepte, S., Reinecke, L. & Behr, K.-M. (2009). Creating virtual alter egos or superheroines? Gamers' strategies of avatar creation in terms of gender and sex. *International Journal of Gaming and Computer-Mediated Simulations*, 1(2), 52–76. doi.org/10.4018/jgcms.2009040104.

Waldron, D. (2005). Role-playing games and the Christian right: Community formation in response to a moral panic. *Journal of Religion and Popular Culture*, 9(1), 3. doi.org/10.3138/jrpc.9.1.003.

Wang, E. S.-T., Chen, L. S.-L., Lin, J. Y.-C. & Wang, M. C.-H. (2008). The relationship between leisure satisfaction and life satisfaction of adolescents concerning online games. *Adolescence*, 43(169), 177–84. PMID: 18447089.

Waśniewska, M. (2020). The red pill, unicorns and white knights: Cultural symbolism and conceptual metaphor in the slang of online incel communities. In B. Lewandowska-Tomaszczyk (Ed.), *Cultural Conceptualizations in Language and Communication* (pp. 65–82). Springer. doi.org/10.1007/978-3-030-42734-4_4.

Wijman, T. (2019). The global games market will generate $152.1 billion in 2019 as the US overtakes China as the biggest market. *Newzoo*. Retrieved from newzoo.com/insights/articles/the-global-games-market-will-generate-152-1-billion-in-2019-as-the-u-s-overtakes-china-as-the-biggest-market/.

Wojtasik, K. (2020). Utøya–Christchurch–Halle. Right-wing extremists' terrorism. *Security Dimensions. International and National Studies,* 33, 84–97. doi.org/10.5604/01.3001.0014.2670.

Wright, T., Boria, E. & Breidenbach, P. (2002). Creative player actions in FPS online video games: Playing Counter-Strike. *Game Studies*, 2(2), 103–123. Retrieved from www.gamestudies.org/0202/wright/.

Zhang, T. & Frederick, C. M. (2018). Busting the myth of the non-social gamer: Comparing friendship quality between gamers and non-gamers. *Proceedings of the Human Factors and Ergonomics Society Annual Meeting*, 62(1), 746. doi.org/10.1177/1541931218621169.

5

Brand lone wolf: The importance of brand narrative in creating extremists

Andrew Hughes

The lone wolf extremist is now the most likely type of terror attack to happen anywhere on earth (Spaaij, 2010). These individuals, though, are hard to predict, as often they have little to no tangible or physical connection with an existing terror group or cell. They identify, usually only in a digital sense, with existing and accepted beliefs, faiths and values, blending into the mainstream. The methods they use in attacks, such as knives, suicide vests and vehicles, mean that they lie below traditional detection methods until the very last second when they carry out attacks.

However, the use of digital communication tools, such as social media and websites, means that the lone wolf is not necessarily that alone, as their interactions, engagement and reinforcement of behaviours now take place within larger packs through online communities of like-minded individuals (Berntzen and Sandberg, 2014). Within this echo chamber, where most content is created by those in the group, the lone wolf not only feels part of a brand community (Hakala et al., 2017), but also believes that they provide value to that community through protecting and defending it against those perceived as likely to destroy or threaten the community's existence.

The brand community lends a form of legitimacy to the individual (Hakala et al., 2017), creating value, and an experiential element that creates a strong resonance and identification between the individual and community. This chapter explores what role a brand community has in the creation of a lone wolf, and how that community validates the behaviour of an individual leading up to, and even after, a terror incident.

Next, the chapter considers how the creation of intense emotional responses towards media may be another important antecedent in the creation of a lone wolf. The relationship between valence and media content in creating intense emotional responses is already well-established, but there is emerging evidence that media type can also be influential (Bolls et al., 2019) and that the valence in video games may influence the adaptation, learning and reinforcement of certain behaviours (Coyne et al., 2018). This concept will be explored in more detail in relation to the motivational role played by media and valence type on creating intense emotional responses in an individual that may turn them into a lone wolf.

Finally, the chapter examines the relationship between the creation and desire of a lone wolf experience, and the role of the brand community, media types and valence in legitimising and validating a lone wolf act. While the lone wolf experience is unique, there are similarities in sensation and adventure-seeking behaviour with those who may undertake risk-taking activities, such as adventure and outdoor pursuits, or even dark or disaster tourism. The chapter will propose a conceptual model of how a lone wolf may seek to calibrate their behaviour and emotional responses with the experiences of others in the brand community, and also those who may have already committed lone wolf acts.

The lone wolf brand – definition, background and context

The lone wolf can be defined as any individual, who is not part of an established terror group, who carries out an act of terror against those they identify as enemies, threats, opponents or persecutors. Acts of terror may not necessarily just be those that are violent, and may also include acts online, such as doxing, denial of service attacks, harassment, trolling or cyber stalking.

The lone wolf is largely male (McCulloch et al., 2019) and, increasingly in many developed parts of the world, can no longer be stereotyped as being from one type of religious background. Instead, lone wolves identify according to the community they feel they are part of. In more recent times this means that they can appear to be someone who is part of the norm (e.g. white collar, good education, good prospects in life, or even, as in the 2015 San Bernardino attack, married), making them very difficult to spot.

However, they are usually likely to feel that they are outsiders to mainstream society, even when it comes to their immediate family and reference groups. They may show little empathy to others whom they target, which might be a sign of an underlying mental health condition, such as the cluster B personality disorder type, seen through borderline narcissistic individuals, or because they are introverted and have had trouble integrating into a mainstream group.

They are also likely to feel that the norm that they are seen to be part of, usually achieved through mirroring the behaviour of people they interact with outside the home, cares little for their existence. Again, these things are not unique: what makes the lone wolf unique is the feeling that they are always up against it – fighting evil alone – in the role of victim hero. This is important when it comes to the lone wolf finding resonance with the messages they search for and view on the internet, or in other places, as they are searching for a fit between their perceived narrative and that of others.

Like most who may be feeling lonely and isolated, they turn to the internet to find a community they can identify with, and find acceptance in. In a way, doing so is one of the first steps in the creation of the lone wolf brand, which is that they consume and experience media content made by that community for that community. It also implicitly demonstrates to the lone wolf how to target individuals digitally because this is exactly what has happened to them.

Brand community and brand equity: Turning extremism into normality

Keller's seminal work on brand equity (Keller, 2003) is relevant in this space as it provides guidance on how a lone wolf brand identifies with an online community. The brand equity models of Aaker (1992, 1996) and Kapferer (2005) are also useful. Keller's model demonstrates that it is about the perceived and real equity, or value, of the brand, even if the brand is an online extremist group, or identifying with one, as in the case of the Christchurch lone wolf. It provides guidance on why, and how, hate can be normal, even fulfilling and sought after, due to the high level of positive emotional feeling it provides. Keller's model and others like it also provide reasons why the lone wolf seeks out similar narratives that complement theirs.

Most brand equity models start with the notion of awareness and salience of a brand providing a perception that helps create the brand identity. Although the different models are split on the exact sequence of what happens next, they agree that, essentially, this identity helps develop the imagery and performance perceptions and expectations of a brand with a person, which then leads to how a person judges and feels about a brand. All these concepts provide the foundation of how much connection, engagement and loyalty, or, in a nutshell, resonance, a person has towards a brand. Resonance with a brand then provides the equity, for both the person and the brand itself, which then becomes a guide on the sustainability and viability of that relationship.

So, the more positive the feelings elicited at each of these steps of the brand equity model, the more likely the person will engage at a higher and more intense level than those who do not have that same resonance. Using this criteria helps to explain why a lone wolf may not only act the way they do, but also how they got there in the first place. Table 5.1 shows how a lone wolf, such as the one in Christchurch, might be created.

Internal value for the lone wolf is not created just through interaction and engagement in social media: it is also achieved through ego and self-actualisation – as in being seen as a hero of the community, even in the sense of competing with others through surpassing the death toll of previous attacks, and then through raising interest towards one of the ultimate user-generated content items, the manifesto of the attacker.

This makes this last step – unique as it is – the pinnacle for many lone wolves, as it also ensures that they are recognised by society as being an individual who carried out a mass-casualty event, adding further equity to their personal brand. The Christchurch attacker noted this by listing previous attacks and conflicts on the weapons he used to carry out the attack as a way of recognising those he perceived as being the brand leaders for his community.

Table 5.1: The lone wolf actor brand equity model

Brand equity steps	Description	Evidenced by
1. Identification and matching	Awareness, searching and salience; laying the foundation stones	Searching for and identifying content, communities and subcultures that closely match the narrative of the individual
2. Building trust – perception and expectations	Perception and imagery; joining a community	Watching and assessing groups or communities and subcultures to ensure that they can trust their decisions and those of the group, perhaps liking and commenting on some posts to see what happens
3. Solidifying	Performance, reinforcement and intensity of feelings; contributing to a community	Seeing what value is offered by different communities and subcultures, and, if these match the feelings sought, adding content internally to obtain group validation and authenticity
4. Resonance	Engagement, community leader brand, connection, networking	Making and sharing content, especially user-made, directly with communities or subcultures of which they are a member; seeking validation and value through likes, comments and shares, especially by other leaders or 'celebrities' in the group
5. Loyalty and ego	Actions in the external community validated by the internal community; high levels of positive emotional feelings	Undertaking targeted actions on those not part of the brand community or subculture, the more harmful and public the better, especially as rated on a scale from local, to national, to global and, finally, to historical; provides value, especially in being seen as a leader for other lone wolves

This is perhaps another reason why it may be difficult to identify the next lone wolf, as this final step in the process – achieving the ultimate ego and adulation within the internal community, and creating fear within the external community – is usually buried deep within the individual until the very moment they decide to carry out a mass-casualty event.

The 'match-up' theory: Content and narrative

The match-up theory means that the lone wolf is seeking to match their narrative with that of others. The closer the match, the more relevant (and, therefore, more viewed, shared and engaged with) content found on the internet becomes.

As Vargo and Lusch (2004) note, this is co-creation of value, whereby two actors exchange something of value that they have helped to create. In this case, the content provider is getting value from views in the form of affirmation that what they have made is being seen by the right audience; for the viewer, the content affirms that their feelings are not unique and that there are many others who feel the same way. This notion may be perhaps assisted by mental illness (Spaaij, 2010), such as cluster B illnesses like borderline personality disorder and narcissism, which Fjotolf Hansen, who carried out the 2011 Norway attacks in Oslo and Utoya Island, may have suffered from.

Either way, the lone wolf is perhaps more vulnerable than others to falling foul of the echo chamber effect of large social media brands, be they open or dark, and thereby of consuming media that reinforces feelings, beliefs and perceptions about the world at large that may not necessarily be so. As the Royal Commission of Inquiry into the Terrorist Attack on Christchurch Masjidain on 15 March 2019 (2020) found, the perpetrator had used YouTube widely in the lead-up to the attack, and had searched for and watched content that closely matched the narrative they had developed about their own life.

But what makes a person move from watching content to carrying out an attack on people peacefully worshipping in a mosque in Christchurch where the youngest victim was only three? This is the where the development of a narrative by the lone wolf that matched the content they viewed needs to be better understood.

For the content to change someone's behaviour to the level where they carried out an attack, it would need to exactly match the narrative that had already been constructed (Solomon et al., 1992; Kamins, 1990). If these did not match, cognitive dissonance could be created within a person, reducing the impact of both the narrative and the content. However, since the content is created by users in a community for other users in that community, dissonance is reduced, and congruence increased, making for a good match between each. This process reinforces the positive, emotional appeal and intensity of positive or rewarding feelings by a lone wolf.

When negative visuals are used, such as that of previous terror attacks, or threats of being harmed, this can magnify the impact even further, as negative images are more likely to elicit deeper emotional feelings and responses, and thus are more likely to be remembered, than positive images (Lang, 1991).

This is essentially what creates the echo chamber effect, as a person is likely to seek reinforcement of perceptions and beliefs through replicating past behaviour, leading to those perceptions and beliefs being formulated. This is likely a key reason why the Christchurch terror suspect watched YouTube: the platform would have provided ready-made menus of content it knew he would like, leading him to spend more time on the platform – a plus for advertisers, of course but not for society.

The algorithm helped to create a nightmare scenario for those who would become part of the worst terror attack in the southern hemisphere, committed by someone who believed that he was acting as a hero in saving the rest of us from a threat that we could not see or comprehend.

Developing the narrative and laying the groundwork: User-generated content

For visual content to be motivationally relevant, and therefore acquire and keep the attention of the person at whom it is targeted, it needs to be connected to a wider narrative that resonates with the viewer (Keller 2003).

As noted earlier, part of this, especially from an effectiveness viewpoint, is community-made content, or user-generated content. User-generated content has been around for centuries, and the use of it as a way of telling stories and building emotional appeals in those who view it can be traced back to the earliest human civilisations. Its power, though, on human behaviour, is linked to authorship. Content made by those in the brand community is far more motivationally relevant than content that is not made by that community. The former type of content is likely to be viewed and remembered far more than content made by other sources, and is therefore likely to have more influence on human behaviour.

The visionary narrative: The manifesto of the victim hero

User-generated content may not necessarily be visual; it can also contain other elements. One type of user-generated content often used by lone wolves, such as in Norway and Christchurch, is the manifesto. A manifesto – created to act as inspiration and motivation for others in the community, to boast of the achievements of the writer and to show brand superiority over other lone wolves – is becoming the norm for those who carry out mass-casualty events. The popularity of this type of content in the far right should come as no surprise considering the enduring popularity of publications such as *Mein Kampf* within these communities.

A manifesto, though, also serves as an important tool for defining a narrative and making the lone wolf distinctive from others who have carried out attacks. The narrative constructed in the document helps to provide validity and reinforcement to the more visual elements of communications that may be shared and viewed by the lone wolf. Importantly, a manifesto provides the logic and rationale to behaviours that are anything but, further reinforcing the perception that the lone wolf is not doing anything evil. In fact, as the victim hero they are only standing up for what is good, and taking on the monsters that the rest of us are not able to fight. Again, this is perhaps another important finding to note, as the perpetrators of recent lone wolf attacks do not tend to see their actions as being wrong, just misunderstood.

The manifesto is representative of so much of what lone wolves seek through content associated with their narrative: the same emotional level and intensity of response from their internal community and reference group that they receive from the external community, but in equally opposite ways. There may be times when both a positive and negative external response is desired by the lone wolf, such as with a mass-casualty event on a targeted group or group of people, but for the main, the lone wolf seeks positive reinforcement from the content they seek, like and make from their community, compared to obtaining positive emotional responses internally through the negative emotional responses and feelings from the external community that they are a part of.

Table 5.2: Key user-generated content items of the lone wolf

Content item	Description	Emotional response desired (influence, impact, reach, emotional response)
Meme	Static image that is usually based on popular images from the internet and adapted with text	Internal – high+ External – low to medium–
Image	Static image usually taken by the creator on a mobile device, sometimes modified for basic enhancements such as text or photo imaging	Internal – high+ External – low to medium–
Manifesto	Written document outlining the vision, values and views of the author, based on their perception of their world	Internal – very high+ External – low to very high–
Video	Usually shot on a mobile phone device, can be first-person point of view, or taken of an incident, person or event	Internal – very high+ External – low to very high–
Social media post (open)	Any post on social media that can be seen by anyone, usually targeted individuals, groups or organisations external to the lone wolf's community or reference group; these types of posts are known as trolling, negging or shit-posting	Internal – very high+ External – very high–
Social media post (closed)	Any post on social media that cannot be seen by others outside the selected audience; will usually include some other type of content to increase impact and response	Internal – very high+ External – none
Website	Usually open to all to see; will carry much of the previous content items, especially the manifesto, and may be more noticeably active in the months leading up to a mass-casualty event	Internal – very high+ External – very high–

The manifesto, though, gives the lone wolf an audience, both pre- and post-event, especially through sharing and seeking out other content they have made, creating a virality effect that, to the lone wolf, is near peak ego and self-actualisation in relation to their behaviour. The audience then becomes like another target, in this case for the content the lone wolf makes, shares, likes and comments on, and eventually even witnesses to what may be a mass-casualty attack, as was seen through the livestreaming of Christchurch by the perpetrator.

A manifesto guides, centres and validates nearly all that the lone wolf does, and to the lone wolf it is a critical part of not only their brand but also their brand activities, both pre- and post-event. If anything, it is usually the most important piece of content made by a lone wolf, as it helps explain their narrative and who they really are.

Visual content, social media and the echo chamber

User-generated content helps the echo chamber effect (Hughes, 2018), helping to create within the lone wolf a feeling of a 'safe' space, a supportive community, but also developing a conditional response emotionally towards content that they see as being supportive of their narrative, and, conversely, content that is to be hated or disliked (Zeki and Romaya, 2008).

The power of images, especially negative ones, to create high levels of arousal in emotional responses helps to move the lone wolf towards action. This power has been well documented in contexts such as television news (Lang et al., 1996), cancer advertisements (Lang, 2006) and news reports (Grabe et al., 2000). And, of course, throughout history the power of negativity to motivate, engage and change behaviour has been acknowledged from the time of the pyramids to the use of images in war recruitment to the propaganda machine of Goebbels in Nazi Germany. More recently, the Trump Presidential campaign of 2016 used negative images, and especially social media platforms such as Facebook and Twitter, as a key part of its campaigning, and then during the presidency. Groups such as QAnon have also helped to make extreme views seem normal, using social media methods to lend validity and credibility to their views. These types of examples illustrate how hate speech is no longer seen as unusual but has become mainstream – even acceptable – to many who, in the past, may have questioned its validity and construct.

The use of iconography, such as tattoos, flags, posters and even brands, by movements has an influential role here as well, as demonstrated in the storming of the US Capitol Building in 2021. In the US and Australian defence forces, the 'Punisher symbol', from the movie and book of the same name, was used by small groups aligned to far-right causes to justify and support their actions and to obtain members.

Iconography not only acts as a signal to others who identify with the movement, but also as a motivator and reinforcer of behaviour. Iconography has been used for centuries by movements. In the modern era, where a movement can start within minutes, it provides a useful identifier to those who may not want formal membership of a group attached to that movement, but instead identify just with the core values and belief of the community engaged with that movement.

Iconography, and its use by lone wolves, be they the person who committed the attack in Christchurch or another individual, has turned hate into an acceptable belief, a form and type of political expression protected by free speech laws, defended as being a stand against political correctness and woke views. Perhaps it needs to be examined with a far more critical eye on the likelihood of that being a sign of someone who may one day be involved with committing a serious atrocity against society?

More recently, the power of visual content has increased because of the move to using visual platforms, such as Facebook, YouTube, Instagram, Snapchat and Pinterest and others, as a way of disseminating information. This may be in response to the growth of an increasingly information-intensive culture and society (Lang, 2006), but it also reflects the fact that visual information is usually easier and quicker to comprehend and understand than non-visual information. A good example of this is the meme factories of lore that have become so well used during nearly every single election in Western democracies since the 2016 US presidential race, in which they became a tool of influence and infamy. Even more recently, emojis are being seen as a way of assisting in the conveyance of information and eliciting recall (Chatzichristos et al., 2020).

These methods have increased the influence of internet platforms that use large amounts of visual information and enable users to curate the content they want, and do not want, to see. Visual content takes seconds to create; even a video filmed in 8K image quality can take under an hour to create, upload and then be ready to be viewed by a potential audience of billions around the globe. Sometimes content filters used by social media brands are incapable of spotting questionable material, which means that it remains viewable for far longer than intended, being seen by who knows how big of an audience before it is taken down and removed. As much as digital media has transformed entire industries, it also has transformed how lone wolves operate and the speed at which they may move from looking at content to acting on it. The use of visual content is also complemented by other forms of content available on social media, such as posts, that help with building equity of the lone wolf.

Make them angry: Hate speech, negging and sh*tposting

Negative content has proven to be more powerful than positive content (Lang et al., 2015), especially when it comes to recall and effect on behaviour and cognition (Nabi, 1996). People with pre-existing mental conditions that make them susceptible to depression and anxiety, a common background trait with lone wolves, are even more likely to recall and be influenced by negative information (Gotlib, 1983).

What this means in the context of the lone wolf is that the use of negative content by them is more likely than not. This may be sometimes hidden by a wider trend in using negative content across society, most notably politics, but it means that it has become a weapon of choice of the lone wolf, as its real motivation can easily be obscured behind subjective lines in a debate.

At times this escalates into more deliberative actions, be it trolling those who are perceived as the enemy or bad people, or undertaking negging behaviour, as in intentionally being harmful through actions such as 'sh*tposting' or posting negative content with the objective of hurting the perceived bad people in the external community. This creates a positive emotional response internally for the lone wolf, usually through negative reactions from the targets and positive responses from the lone wolf's internal community. This conditions the lone wolf into a cycle where they see their posts, and the ones they like, comment or share, as being part of standing up for the good of the cause and society, and the negative responses as proof that their targets are indeed the right ones due to the nature and intensity of their responses.

In a way, these methods become part of the operating policies of the lone wolf, be they current or future, as they feed into the broader narrative that the lone wolf is building, of them being the victim hero in a society blind to what they see. Unwinding this mess is not as simple as stopping the posts on social media, even though that would help significantly, but is also connected to the perception of the lone wolf, which may be influenced by a pre-existing mental health condition, diagnosed or not. Negging helps the lone wolf justify their behaviour. Understanding the effect of these behaviours can help researchers understand the role of user-generated visual content in constructing the narrative of the victim hero.

Conclusion

Lone wolf terror attacks are increasing throughout the world, but especially in the United States and other Western nations. The lone wolf, though, does not see themselves as being radicalised. They instead see content, iconography and visual information that reinforces the belief that they are good, doing their community and us a favour by killing those who threaten our way of life. That is the power of visual communication – to make us believe something to be true that is not.

To change this there needs to be changes to algorithms on violent and extremist content on social media sites, on how search engines produce results that may assist those looking for a match-up with their behaviour with what they can find online, so that they feel that they are normal and it is we who are the ones living as outliers.

Visual communication methods are providing the lone wolf with validation at the individual and community level: individually through reinforcement of behaviours; at the community level through engagement and connection with others to share content, ideas and methods, and via competition over the power of their manifesto and narrative.

Reducing visual content online is problematic and may push it into spaces on the internet where there is no light. Yet, to allow it to exist only further increases the chances that others will one day move from just having an interest to actually taking the lives of innocent people in the name of loyalty to brands and movements that most of us have no identification with.

A easier solution is to change how the content is found and the underlying reasons for its emotional relevance to people who should see hope but instead only see darkness. To the lone wolf, darkness is love, a familiarity that provides comfort, but, sadly, for the rest of us, only gives nightmares and loss. In the digital age, though, with the normalisation of violence, hate and aggression, and ease of access to information and content to reinforce a co-created narrative, lone wolf attacks are growing in number and intensity. But this does not mean we should give up, because the power is in each of us to change the narrative and thereby change the end on the story of the lone wolf.

References

Aaker, D. A. (1992). The value of brand equity. *Journal of Business Strategy*, 13(4), 27–32. doi.org/10.1108/eb039503.

Aaker, D. A. (1996). Measuring brand equity across products and markets. *California Management Review*, 38(3), 102–20.

Berntzen, L. E. & Sandberg, S. (2014). The collective nature of lone wolf terrorism: Anders Behring Breivik and the anti-Islamic social movement. *Terrorism and Political Violence*, 26(5), 759–79. doi.org/10.1080/09546553. 2013.767245.

Bolls, P. D., Weber, R., Lang, A., Potter, R. F., Oliver, M. B., Raney, A. A. & Jennings, B. (2019). Media psychophysiology and neuroscience. In M. B. Oliver, A. A. Raney & J. Bryant (Eds), *Media Effects: Advances In Theory And Research*. Routledge. doi.org/10.4324/9780429491146-13.

Chatzichristos, C., Morante, M., Andreadis, N., Kofidis, E., Kopsinis, Y. & Theodoridis, S. (2020). Emojis influence autobiographical memory retrieval from reading words: An fMRI-based study. *PLoS ONE*, 15(7). doi. org/10.1371/journal.pone.0234104.

Coyne, S. M., Warburton, W. A., Essig, L. W. & Stockdale, L. A. (2018). Violent video games, externalizing behaviour, and prosocial behaviour: A five-year longitudinal study during adolescence. *Developmental Psychology*, 54(10), 1868–80. doi.org/10.1037/dev0000574.

Gotlib, I. H. (1983). Perception and recall of interpersonal feedback: Negative bias in depression. *Cognitive Therapy and Research*, 7(5), 399–412. doi.org/10.1007/BF01187168.

Grabe, M. E., Lang, A., Zhou, S. & Bolls, P. D. (2000). Cognitive access to negatively arousing news: An experimental investigation of the knowledge gap. *Communication Research*, 27(1), 3–26. doi.org/10.1177/009365000027001001.

Hakala, H., Niemi, L. & Kohtamäki, M. (2017). Online brand community practices and the construction of brand legitimacy. *Marketing Theory*, 17(4), 537–58. doi.org/10.1177/1470593117705695.

Hughes, A. (2018). *Market Driven Political Advertising: Social, Digital and Mobile Marketing.* Springer. doi.org/10.1007/978-3-319-77730-6.

Kamins, M. A. (1990). An investigation into the 'match-up' hypothesis in celebrity advertising: When beauty may be only skin deep. *Journal of Advertising*, 19(1), 4–13. doi.org/10.1080/00913367.1990.10673175.

Kapferer, J. N. (2005). The two business cultures of luxury brands. In J. Schroeder & M. Salzer Morling (Eds). *Brand Culture* (pp. 67–76). London: Routledge. doi.org/10.4324/9780203002445.

Keller, K. L. (2003). Brand synthesis: The multidimensionality of brand knowledge. *Journal of Consumer Research*, 29(4), 595–600. doi.org/10.1086/346254.

Lang, A. (1991). Emotion, formal features, and memory for televised political advertisements. *Television and Political Advertising*, 1(1), 221–43.

Lang, A. (2006). Using the limited capacity model of motivated mediated message processing to design effective cancer communication messages. *Journal of Communication*, 56, S57–S80. doi.org/10.1111/j.1460-2466.2006.00283.x.

Lang, A., Bailey, R. L. & Connolly, S. R. (2015). Encoding systems and evolved message processing: Pictures enable action, words enable thinking. *Media and Communication*, 3(1), 34–43. doi.org/10.17645/mac.v3i1.248.

Lang, A., Newhagen, J. & Reeves, B. (1996). Negative video as structure: Emotion, attention, capacity, and memory. *Journal of Broadcasting & Electronic Media*, 40(4), 460–77. doi.org/10.1080/08838159609364369.

McCulloch, J., Walklate, S., Maher, J., Fitz-Gibbon, K. & McGowan, J. (2019). Lone wolf terrorism through a gendered lens: Men turning violent or violent men behaving violently? *Critical Criminology*, 27(3), 437–50. doi.org/10.1007/s10612-019-09457-5.

Nabi, R. L. (1999). A cognitive-functional model for the effects of discrete negative emotions on information processing, attitude change, and recall. *Communication Theory*, 9(3), 292–320. doi.org/10.1111/j.1468-2885.1999.tb00172.x.

Royal Commission of Inquiry into the Terrorist Attack on Christchurch Masjidain on 15 March 2019. (2020, 26 November). *Report.* Retrieved from christchurchattack.royalcommission.nz/the-report/.

Solomon, M. R., Ashmore, R. D. & Longo, L. C. (1992). The beauty match-up hypothesis: Congruence between types of beauty and product images in advertising. *Journal of Advertising*, 21(4), 23–34. doi.org/10.1080/0091336 7.1992.10673383.

Spaaij, R. (2010). The enigma of lone wolf terrorism: An assessment. *Studies in Conflict & Terrorism*, 33(9), 854–70. doi.org/10.1080/1057610x.2010.501426.

Vargo, S. L. & Lusch, R. F. (2004). Evolving to a new dominant logic for marketing. *Journal of Marketing*, 68(1), 1–17. doi.org/10.1509/jmkg.68.1.1.24036.

Zeki, S. & Romaya, J. P. (2008). Neural correlates of hate. *PLoS ONE*, 3(10). doi.org/10.1371/journal.pone.0003556.

6

'Clumsy and flawed in many respects': Australia's abhorrent violent material legislation[1]

Mark Nolan and Dominique Dalla-Pozza

Introduction

An alarming feature of the Christchurch mosque attacks was the fact that the perpetrator went not only armed, but also rigged up with a camera to fulfil his plan of livestreaming the attacks on the internet. In addition to the writing of a manifesto and the detailed planning of the attack itself, the attacker successfully fulfilled his intention of broadcasting the attack on the internet. As described by Douek (2020, p. 41):

---

1   This chapter was initially developed and presented for the symposium 'After Christchurch: Violent Extremism Online' hosted by the ANU Australian Studies Institute and held at the ANU College of Law, Canberra, on 29 August 2019. A form of this paper was presented at the Joint Conference of the Australian and New Zealand Association of Psychiatry, Psychology and Law and the Forensic Faculty of the Royal Australian and New Zealand College of Psychiatry, Collaboration and Challenges Across the Global South, held in Singapore on 5–8 November 2019. The authors also made a submission (submission 15) to the Parliamentary Joint Committee on Law Enforcement inquiry on the *Criminal Code Amendment (Sharing of Abhorrent Violent Material) Act 2019* in November 2021, which drew upon the material in this chapter. See www.aph.gov.au/Parliamentary_Business/Committees/Joint/ Law_Enforcement/AVMAct/Submissions.

> When the shooter entered the Christchurch mosques on Friday
> 15 March 2019, he was armed not only with guns but also with
> a helmet camera that streamed the attack live on Facebook. For the
> next 16 minutes and 55 seconds, the footage of his horrific violence
> was broadcast around the world in real time on Facebook Live.

In the aftermath of this broadcast the Australian Government acted
swiftly and exceptionally to pass the *Criminal Code Amendment (Sharing
of Abhorrent Violent Material) Act 2019* (Cth) in an attempt to reduce the
risk of broadcasting such terrorist attacks in the future. In this chapter
we are critical of the way in which this legislative desire was achieved,
arguably in pursuit of a very noble aim to avoid the additional suffering
that was caused by the broadcast of such horrendous attacks.

Our criticisms centre firstly around the unusual features of the legislative
process used at this time, in the lead-up to an election, particularly the
lack of parliamentary debate and the absence of committee consideration;
and, secondly, the nature of the regulatory regime created, implicating an
arguably under-resourced and under-prepared eSafety commissioner, and
its links to problematic offence definition. There are some controversial
ways of establishing the fault elements in some of the new offences
created. These concerns resonate with the surprised reactions of some
other commentators (e.g. Douek, 2020) who, like us, worry about the
potentially negative consequences of yet another piece of hastily drafted
and powerful counterterrorism law affecting both telecommunications
and internet companies and individuals alike.

Process problems with the passage of the *Criminal Code Amendment (Sharing of Abhorrent Violent Material) Act 2019* (Cth)

Little substantive parliamentary debate

An analysis of the parliamentary debate of the *Criminal Code Amendment
(Sharing of Abhorrent Violent Material) Act 2019* (the *AVM Act*) reveals
a number of striking features. The first is that the legislation was
explicitly framed as a direct response to the shootings in Christchurch.
Attorney-General Christian Porter opened substantive debate on the Bill
'by paying tribute to all those who suffered and lost their lives and lost

loved ones as a result of the Christchurch terrorist attack' (Commonwealth, 2019a, p. 1849). He then moved to argue that the AVM Bill was required to address two infamous features of the Christchurch attack: the livestreaming of the shooting on social media and the fact that that recording was available for viewing or download on those platforms for over an hour (Commonwealth, 2019a, p. 1849; Douek, 2020, p. 45). As the attorney-general said, 'we must act to ensure that perpetrators [of terrorist acts] and their accomplices cannot leverage online platforms for the purposes of spreading their violent and extreme … propaganda' (Commonwealth, 2019a, p. 1849; see also Commonwealth, 2019b, paragraph 2).

A similar structure is observable in the opening comments by non-government parliamentarians who contributed to debate in the House of Representatives. Shadow Attorney-General Mark Dreyfus acknowledged '[t]he terrorist atrocity committed in New Zealand' (Commonwealth, 2019c, p. 1851) and then moved to outlining the Opposition position: 'Labor believes that social media companies must do more in preventing the dissemination of material produced by terrorists showing off their crimes' and therefore the Opposition would support the Bill 'despite reservations' (Commonwealth, 2019c, p. 1852). The Australian Greens indicated that '[w]e all grieve with New Zealand' (Commonwealth, 2019d, p. 1855) and signalled that their party had previously advocated for more legislative changes in relation to social media (Commonwealth, 2019d, p. 1856). Independent MP Kerryn Phelps directly called the events in Christchurch a 'catalyst' for the legislation (Commonwealth, 2019e, p. 1857).

While the explicit linking of the AVM Bill with the events in Christchurch was a noticeable feature of the parliamentary process, it was not an unusual one. It is reasonably common for pieces of Australia's (now complex) counterterrorism law framework to be developed or adjusted in reaction to various terrorist atrocities (Lynch et al., 2015, pp. 198–200, Blackbourn et al., 2019, pp. 186–87). For example, the terrorist attacks in the US on 11 September 2001 catalysed major Australian counterterrorism law reform as did the London bombings of 2005 (Lynch et al., 2015, p. 198). Indeed, as one of us has written, the experience of counterterrorism law-making since 2001 means it is likely that substantial amendments to Australia's counterterrorism laws will be made 'in the shadow of a crisis' (Dalla-Pozza, 2016, pp. 272, 278). While there are many reasons why legislators should choose to alter legislation in response to events such as the Christchurch massacre, law-making in such circumstances carries particular challenges (Dalla-Pozza, 2016, p. 282; Lynch et al., 2015, pp. 195–205).

One such challenge is that the time that parliament has to debate these laws can be significantly shortened. The AVM Bill is an especially egregious example of this phenomenon. The Bill was introduced in the Senate on 3 April 2019, mere weeks after the events in Christchurch. As events transpired, 3 April was also the last sitting day when the Senate could consider legislation before the parliament was prorogued prior to the 2019 election (Parliament of Australia, 2019). There was controversy about the 2019 parliamentary sitting calendar with the Labor Opposition claiming that the Morrison Coalition government was seeking to minimise the ability of parliament to provide scrutiny (see Belot, 2018). Some of the background to the 2019 election, including the events that led to the Morrison government lacking an absolute majority in the House of Representatives by early 2019, are usefully summarised by Muller (2020, pp. 3–4). The Senate Hansard for that day records the fact that the events in Christchurch were discussed on this day (see e.g. Commonwealth, 2019f, p. 828). However, there was almost no discussion of the AVM Bill itself. Indeed, while the Hansard indicates that the Bill passed through all the stages formally required, no substantive debate on the Bill is recorded (Commonwealth, 2019f, pp. 992–93). The Bill then moved to the House of Representatives where it was introduced and debated on 4 April. Again, this was the last day that the House had to consider legislation. Just under one hour was spent debating the legislation before it was passed (Commonwealth, 2019g, pp. 1849–60). This only allowed for contributions from four members of parliament: the attorney-general (Christian Porter), the shadow attorney-general (Mark Dreyfus), the leader of the Australian Greens (Adam Bandt) and an independent (Kerryn Phelps). The Bill was given Royal Assent, the final stage required before it became law, on the following day.

It should be recognised that it is impossible to put forward blanket prescriptions of how much time parliament *should* spend publicly considering legislative proposals. Parliamentary time does need to be used appropriately (Uhr, 1998, pp. 124–25, 219–21; Lynch, 2006, p. 779). The amount of consideration time each piece of legislation receives can be influenced by a number of factors (Dalla-Pozza, 2010, pp. 157–58). However, we would argue that the *AVM Act* required more sustained parliamentary attention than it received. As Douek observes, 'writing laws to create social media reform is hard and involves difficult trade-offs'. She mentions the particular complexity of ensuring that 'freedom of expression' is not unduly curtailed by such laws (Douek, 2020, p. 42). However, as will be outlined below, this is only one of the many issues that underpin the *AVM Act*. Douek (2020) also notes that the Morrison government announced that the AVM Bill was 'a world first' (Douek, 2020, p. 42). This suggests that the legislation was novel, as well as being complex. As such, it is difficult to accept that a public law-making process that took place over a mere three-day period (from 3–5 April 2019), and that afforded parliamentarians less than one hour of substantive debate on the features of the Bill, is adequate or appropriate.

Absence of scrutiny by the Parliamentary Joint Committee on Intelligence and Security (PJCIS)

Another striking feature of the parliamentary process that produced the *AVM Act* was the absence of parliamentary committee scrutiny of this legislation. The shadow attorney-general remarked upon the fact that the Bill had not been referred to the PJCIS (Commonwealth, 2019c, p. 1852) and the Greens MP even tried to move an amendment attempting to refer the Bill to that committee, an amendment that was voted down (Commonwealth, 2019d, p. 1856; Commonwealth, 2019f, pp. 1858–60). There is no binding requirement that a piece of law directed to countering terrorism or national security *must* be referred to this committee. Nevertheless, recent assessments of the work of the PJCIS suggest that it is unusual for a piece of legislation like the *AVM Act* to be passed without this committee having the opportunity to scrutinise it. In 2018 Moulds commented that since 2013 the PJCIS 'has inquired into and reported … on each of the key legislative reforms' that related to counterterrorism and national security law (Moulds, 2018, p. 287). Similarly, in the recently released *Comprehensive Review of the Legal Framework of the National Intelligence Community*, Richardson commented that '[i]t is usual practice for Bills relating to national security to be referred' to that committee (Richardson, 2019, p. 21).

The most obvious explanation for the absence of PJCIS scrutiny of the AVM Bill lies in the fact that there was the clear expectation that the parliament would be prorogued prior to an election within days of the AVM Bill being introduced (Commonwealth, 2019c, pp. 1852, 1854). If the Morrison government had referred the AVM Bill to the PJCIS it may have delayed the passage of the Bill, and, in these circumstances, probably have ensured that the Bill would not have been passed before the 2019 election. It is also true that the *AVM Act* contains a provision that mandates some review of the provisions contained within it. The Act itself specified that, two years after these new provisions commenced, 'the Minister must cause to be conducted a review of the operation' of the provisions (s. 474.45). This report needed to be given to the minister within a year after it commenced, and the report needed also to be tabled in the parliament. In fact, the Parliamentary Joint Committee on Law Enforcement was tasked by the attorney-general to complete this review. This committee completed its report on the Act in late 2021 (Parliamentary Joint Committee on Law Enforcement, 2021, p. 1). To the best of our knowledge, at the time of writing, there is no public document outlining the government's response to this review (Parliamentary Joint Committee on Law Enforcement, 2022).

Despite some review process being included, the impact of the absence of expected parliamentary committee scrutiny for this Bill *prior* to its passage should not be underestimated. One of the key criticisms of the *AVM Act* that emerges from both the limited parliamentary debate (Commonwealth, 2019e, p. 1858; Commonwealth, 2019c, p. 1854), and from initial academic consideration of the Act, is that in producing the Act '[t]he government did not consult with experts, civil society or industry' (Douek, 2020, p. 42). Definitely, as suggested by Douek, there was no connection or reference to the ongoing work being completed by the *Australian Taskforce to Combat Terrorist and Extreme Violent Material Online*, which reported only a few months after the Christchurch bombings (Douek, 2020, p. 58).

There are two main problems associated with this lack of consultation. Firstly, as will be further discussed, there were many complex aspects of this Bill. It is possible that if a parliamentary committee such as the PJCIS were allowed to scrutinise the Bill, and call for submissions from non-government entities or scholars, alternative ways of responding to the challenge of using the criminal law to regulate the appearance and spread of abhorrent violent material online could have been devised.

Secondly, in denying the PJCIS an opportunity to consider the AVM Bill before it was enacted, the parliament was not making full use of its 'deliberative capacities' (Uhr, 1998, p. 92; Dalla-Pozza, 2016, p. 273). This is significant because ensuring that the parliament functions more as a deliberative democratic assembly is one way in which to measure whether an appropriate 'balance' has been struck between the competing considerations that underpin counterterrorism legislation more generally (Dalla-Pozza, 2016, pp. 274–75).

These deficiencies of the parliamentary process were a key theme of the contributions from non-government MPs, despite the fact that there was still support for the Bill from those outside of the government, perhaps an indication that all politicians had already begun to be in election mode. While the shadow attorney-general was in the difficult position of having to argue that the Opposition would support the rushed passage of the laws (Commonwealth, 2019c, p. 1853), he also maintained that there needed to be 'proper consultation' in relation to the Bill, mentioning that the AVM Bill may not only impact the 'social media sector' but 'traditional media' as well (Commonwealth, 2019c, p. 1854). Greens MP Adam Bandt opined that 'because … [the Bill] is being rushed through', the parliament does not:

> Know whether or not the bill in fact does the job the Attorney-General tells us it is doing … we do not know whether or not it goes far enough in stopping that kind of hate speech from being broadcast. (Commonwealth, 2019d, p. 1855)

Similarly, independent Kerryn Phelps commented that 'laws formulated as a knee jerk reaction to a tragic event do not necessarily equate to good legislation and can have myriad unintended consequences' (Commonwealth, 2019e, p. 1858). She speculated that one such 'unintended consequence' was that international IT companies may avoid Australia to ensure that they are not caught by the *AVM Act* (Commonwealth, 2019e, p. 1858). This relates to the confident assertion of extraterritorial jurisdiction relating to the offences defined in the Bill.

One of the interesting things about these contributions from parliamentarians is that they illuminate the point that there is a connection between the content of a law and the parliamentary process that produced it. Over the last 20 years, a distinct strand of scholarship that focuses on the connection between legislative processes and the content of specific laws has emerged (see e.g. Lynch, 2006, p. 779; Lynch et al., 2015, p. 198; Carne, 2016, p. 5). It seems clear that the *AVM Act* was the product of a process that was truly 'clumsy and flawed' in many respects (see also

Douek, 2020, p. 60). The following section will examine in more detail the *content* of the Act and some of the exceptional and problematic aspects of the 'offence' definition and related regulatory features of the Bill.

Problems related to the offences created by the Act

In support of and in addition to the important concerns listed by Douek (2020), relating to offence definition or otherwise, we would like to highlight the following matters relating to the content of the Act. This Act is a controversial gap-filling exercise alongside existing cybercrime laws that impose liability for the terrorist offender for also posting material online; that there may not be a high threshold for material to meet the definition of abhorrent violent material; and that there is a tension between proof of subjective fault offences and liability proved via objective fact only, that should concern defence lawyers engaged by providers. First, a brief overview of what offences and defences are created by the *AVM Act* is in order. We can also note here statements about liability and exposure to notification and prosecutorial powers that have been made publicly by the eSafety commissioner herself. Here, she speaks of the potential impact of the new powers thrust upon her at very short notice, requiring much work by her office, following passage of this Bill in April 2019. Some of her other statements update us about how those new powers have been exercised to date.

The new provisions

Definitions

The definitions provided in the *AVM Act* are detailed and are of crucial importance to evaluating the potential impact of the new offences created. To begin with, but also avoiding in-depth discussion that these complex definitional provisions deserve, we note that relevant definitions can now be found in s. 474.30 of the *Criminal Code* (Cth), defining, via an exhaustive 'means' definition, that a 'content service' is a 'social media service' (within the meaning of the *Enhancing Online Safety Act 2015* (Cth)) or a 'designated internet service' (within the meaning of the *Enhancing Online Safety Act 2015* (Cth)). Similarly, a 'hosting service' has the same meaning as in the *Enhancing Online Safety Act 2015* (Cth) but excludes subparagraphs 9C(a)(ii) and (b)(ii) of that Act.

Importantly, the focus of the *AVM Act* is clearly on the blameworthiness of those *content service providers* and *hosting service providers*, and, clearly, not *internet service providers* (ISPs) or 'providers of relevant electronic services such as chat and instant messaging services' as noted in paragraph [8] of the Explanatory Memorandum to the Bill (Commonwealth, 2019b, p. 6).

The Act provides definitions for 'abhorrent violent conduct' (AVC) and 'abhorrent violent material' (AVM) in the new Subdivision H ('Offences relating to the use of carriage service for the sharing of abhorrent violent material') of Division 474 ('Communications Offences') in the *Criminal Code* (Cth). The latter relies on the former for its meaning.

The definition of AVM, now found in s. 474.31 of the *Criminal Code* (Cth), states the following, via another exhaustive 'means' definition:

474.31 Abhorrent violent material

1. For the purposes of this Subdivision, **abhorrent violent material** means material that:

   a. is:
      i. audio material; or
      ii. visual material; or
      iii. audio-visual material;

      that records or streams abhorrent violent conduct engaged in by one or more persons; and

   b. is material that reasonable persons would regard as being, in all the circumstances, offensive; and

   c. is produced by a person who is, or by 2 or more persons each of whom is:
      i. a person who engaged in the abhorrent violent conduct; or
      ii. a person who conspired to engage in the abhorrent violent conduct; or
      iii. a person who aided, abetted, counselled or procured, or was in any way knowingly concerned in, the abhorrent violent conduct; or
      iv. a person who attempted to engage in the abhorrent violent conduct.

2. For the purposes of this section, it is immaterial whether the material has been altered.

3. For the purposes of this section, it is immaterial whether the abhorrent violent conduct was engaged in within or outside Australia.

It is worth noting here that what makes the material 'abhorrent', it seems, is the definitional element in s. 474.31(1)(b), namely, that the audio material, visual material or audio-visual material that records or streams abhorrent violent conduct engaged in by one or more persons (s. 474.31(1)(a)), *and* is material that reasonable persons would regard as being, in all the circumstances, offensive. This objective reasonable-person test, qualified by noting the contextual circumstances, resonates with the objective tests for cyber offensiveness that has been used in relation to the pre-existing s. 474.17 *Criminal Code* (Cth) offence of using a carriage service to menace, harass or cause offence (see below).

The definition of AVC, now found in s. 474.32 of the *Criminal Code* (Cth), is notably much broader than merely including terrorist act offences, defined to be the same as in s. 100.1 of the *Criminal Code* (Cth) excluding paragraphs 100.1(2)(b), (d), (e) and (f). Interestingly, the *AVM Act* includes a much broader range of offences in its definition of AVC, so, it was a net-widening opportunity to respond to more than the features of the Christchurch attack livestreaming alone:

474.32 Abhorrent violent conduct

1. For the purposes of this Subdivision, a person engages in abhorrent violent conduct if the person:
   a. engages in a terrorist act; or
   b. murders another person; or
   c. attempts to murder another person; or
   d. tortures another person; or
   e. rapes another person; or
   f. kidnaps another person.

In order to work with all elements of these definitions, and offence types further defined within the *AVM Act*, a rather detailed knowledge of some of the most complex criminal offences defined in the *Criminal Code* (Cth), or elsewhere, is required. This places an enormous burden upon not only staff in the Office of the eSafety Commissioner, but also upon the lawyers or others within companies, community organisations or other groups and upon any individuals providing content and hosting services. Anyone assessing the content of internet postings must possess an understanding of whether the material in question represents criminal liability, not only for terrorism, which would be challenging enough to assess, but also for four other types of criminal offence, including what it means to attempt murder.

Offences

Two new offences are created by the *AVM Act*.

The failure to notify offence

The first offence defined under s. 474.33 of the *Criminal Code* (Cth) is a failure to notify offence, placed upon a provider located anywhere in the world (a form of extraterritoriality that again involves a broad investigative and regulatory scope with extensive resource implications). It criminalises awareness that the AVM can be accessed by a service that the defendant manages when they have reasonable grounds to believe that the AVM material is recording or streaming AVC that has or is occurring in Australia (at least that requirement is some form of geographical limit here), and when the defendant individual or organisation/company does not refer the existence of that AVM to Australian Federal Police (AFP) within a 'reasonable time'. A similar failure to notify offence already existed in the *Criminal Code* (Cth) under s. 474.25 in relation to child pornography and child abuse material on the internet, albeit with considerably less serious maximum penalties.

Crucially, no further definition of 'reasonable time' is given. There is some further detail about this provided in the Explanatory Memorandum but there will still be a need for parties to any prosecution to debate what 'reasonable time means' when that is applied to the specific facts of failure to notify behaviour:

> A 'reasonable time' is not defined. A number of factors and circumstances could indicate whether a person had referred details of abhorrent violent material within a reasonable time after becoming aware of the existence of the material. For example, the *type and volume of the material*, and the *capabilities of and resourcing available to the provider may be relevant factors*. In a prosecution for an offence against section 474.33, the determination of whether

material was referred within a reasonable time will be a matter for the trier of fact. (Commonwealth, 2019b, p. 19, paragraph [39], emphasis added)

It is encouraging here, in the interests of potential defendants, that resourcing available to the provider is listed as a potential reason to shape the definition of 'reasonable time', perhaps allowing that time to be defined as longer than may otherwise be the case for better-resourced providers.

This offence carries a maximum penalty of a fine of $168,000 for natural persons and a fine of $840,000 for corporations (Commonwealth, 2019b, p. 19, paragraph [40]). As with some similar decisions to charge individuals and corporations, including those based overseas, with *Criminal Code* (Cth) offences, the attorney-general needs to give written consent before 'proceedings' can begin under s. 474.33 if the conduct that is alleged to constitute an offence under the section occurs entirely overseas *and* the individual charged is *not* an Australian citizen or the corporation involved is not incorporated under Australian law (under 47442(1)) but arrests can be made prior to that consent to charge being given (s. 474.42(2)) (see also Douek, 2020, pp. 43).

The failure to remove offence

The second offence created under s. 474.34 of the *Criminal Code* (Cth) criminalises the failure of relevant providers based anywhere in the world to effect 'expeditious removal' of AVM able to be accessed within Australia. Subjective fault elements of recklessness are provided by the drafters of this offence as attaching to the physical elements of whether the material is AVM and whether the material can be accessed within Australia. The usual relevant federal criminal law definition of subjective recklessness under s 5.4 of the *Criminal Code* (Cth) that would normally apply here for individuals would be:

5.4 (1) A person is reckless with respect to a circumstance if:

a. he or she is aware of a substantial risk that the circumstance exists or will exist; and

b. having regard to the circumstances known to him or her, it is unjustifiable to take the risk.

For corporations, the detailed provisions set out in Part 2.5 of the *Criminal Code* (Cth) would normally apply, allowing recklessness of a corporation to be proved more indirectly from a range of organisational dynamics including corporate culture (Clough, 2007; Clough, 2017; Clough and Mulhern, 2002).

The removal expected would render it inaccessible to end users of the service (s. 474.34(15)). Again, the crucial temporal element of 'expeditious' was not defined in the *AVM Act* (see also Douek, 2020, pp. 45–46, 49) but there is speculation within the Explanatory Memorandum that may assist interpretation of that physical element of the offence when it comes the time for that debate to be had at trial:

> [51] 'Expeditious' is not defined and would be *determined by the trier of fact taking account of all of the circumstances in each case.* A number of factors and circumstances could indicate whether a person had ensured the expeditious removal of the material. For example, the *type and volume of the abhorrent violent material, or the capabilities of and resourcing available to the provider may be relevant factors.* (Commonwealth, 2019b, p. 19, paragraph [51], emphasis added)

It is again reassuring that there will need to be a debate between parties to a prosecution about the relevant definition of 'expeditious' that would apply to a particular case, though the lack of definition here again speaks to a gap left by absent scrutiny of and consultation on one of the more important aspects of the offence definition before passage of the legislation. These are matters that we would normally expect quite rigorous debate upon during a parliamentary debate of greater length.

The penalties for this offence are more severe than for the failure to notify offence, with individuals being liable to a maximum penalty of three years imprisonment or around a $2.1 million fine or both, corporations being liable for the greater of around $10.5 million or 10 per cent of their annual turnover during the 12-month period up to the end of the month within which the offence occurred (s. 474.34). Interestingly, the attorney-general's written consent is needed for charging (s. 474. 42(3)) penalties, but arrests may occur before that consent is given (s. 474.42(4)).

Defences

Defences provided by the *AVM Act* in ss. 474.37–474.38 to the offence provisions cover a range of people including journalists, law enforcement agencies, public officials, researchers, political advocates (protected by a recitation of the implied constitutional freedom of political communication) or artists who may have copied the AVM before it was taken down. These are important protections for a range of people needing to access and share AVM portraying regulated AVC (but see the concerns raised by Douek, 2020, pp. 53, 57).

What the *AVM Act* adds to existing cybercrime laws

It is useful to note from the outset that the *AVM Act* did not provide any new powers or any new creative regulatory ideas about preventing or prosecuting terrorists who plan to livestream their attacks on the internet or otherwise publish AVM on the internet. The attorney-general explained in his Explanatory Memorandum to the Bill that the intention of the drafters of the Bill was to:

> Address significant gaps in Australia's current criminal laws by ensuring that persons who are internet service providers, or who provide content or hosting services, take timely action in relation to abhorrent violent material that can be accessed using their services. This will ensure that online platforms cannot be exploited and weaponised by perpetrators of violence. (Commonwealth, 2019b, para [2])

To clarify, the new provisions do not attempt to regulate the sharing of abhorrent violent material (AVM) via new and targeted cybercrimes that criminalise the specific posting of AVM by a lone actor terrorist or any other person or terrorist group. That potential liability seems already covered by the intersecting web of federal cybercrime offences that had existed for considerable time pre-Christchurch. Such cybercrime laws, for example, include the s. 474.17 offence of using a carriage service to menace, harass or cause offence (where offensiveness is what the reasonable person in all the circumstances would consider offensive as provided by s. 474.17(1)b; see *Crowther v. Sala* [2007] QCA 133 for an in-depth discussion of the offensiveness test and other elements of that offence; and *Waterstone v R* [2020] NSWCCA 117 for a recent application of such a test). Furthermore, the s. 474.15 offence of using a carriage service to make a threat, and the s. 474.14 offence of using a telecommunications network with intention to commit a serious offence, for example, any federal terrorism act or terrorist organisation, or preparation of terrorism offence (or other AVC), could be used against the person who livestreams or posts the AVM to the internet in the first instance.

Attempted reassurance given by the eSafety commissioner

The eSafety commissioner notes in her factsheet (eSafety Commissioner, 2020) that the federal government held a meeting *after the Christchurch attacks* with digital services and ISPs regarding AVM, and with industry stakeholders *after the legislation was passed* to workshop the process for sending and receiving notices, and with 'smaller and mid-tier platforms hosted overseas to establish contacts and escalation paths and advise a broader range of companies about the AVM scheme' (eSafety Commissioner, 2020). Helpfully, the commissioner suggests in her factsheet that ahead of issuing an AVM notice, informal contact can be made with services to notify them unofficially that material is likely to violate that platform's own community standards.

Beyond this attempt to show preparedness by the eSafety commissioner to walk with stakeholders during this regulatory journey, the point can be made that even this level of consultation, engaged in following the passage of the legislation as well as after the attacks and before the parliamentary 'debate', is limited and only goes so far, as Douek (2020) argues. This level of consultation may not have engaged with many smaller scale or currently unknown content service providers and hosting service providers without profile in the industry and without strong and ongoing existing relationships with the commissioner.

In this sense, this level of consultation may have come far too late and may have only reached a small fraction of affected persons, companies and groups. It may contextualise only a small subset of those potentially affected by the possible exercise of the eSafety commissioner's discretion. Even these attempts may mean that many smaller providers could remain under-educated, potentially unknown to the eSafety commissioner, and exposed more easily to damaging potential liability under this new regime. Monitoring the exercise of discretion by the eSafety commissioner and the Commonwealth director of public prosecutions is integral to revealing if there is overreach of these new provisions in prosecutions against smaller providers. A review of the Annual Report of the Commonwealth Director of Public Prosecutions and case analysis over time will reveal if the prosecution rates against content and hosting service providers are problematic.

The eSafety commissioner's factsheet published on 24 March 2020 notes further that there were, up to that time, 18 notices issued to:

> 10 worst-of-the-worst underground gore sites and services that host these sites. The material showed beheadings, shootings and other murders. The notices prompted the removal of 70 per cent of this material. (eSafety Commissioner, 2020)

In that factsheet, apparently aimed at appeasing concerned content and hosting service providers, the eSafety commissioner attempts to reassure all that her powers will only be used 'in the most extreme cases … [and that the commissioner] does not monitor the internet for AVM and it is predominantly a complaints-based regime' (eSafety Commissioner, 2020). The fact that there are no resources to attempt the style of systematic monitoring of the internet that seems assumed by the powers given by the *AVM Act* is of no particular reassurance to those who will become potentially liable under it. In the same factsheet, the commissioner suggests that she: 'assesses material on a case-by-case basis, using discretion to determine whether it is appropriate to issue a notice. This is not a heavy-handed approach' (eSafety Commissioner, 2020). Despite those attempts to reassure all that the commissioner is reluctant to use her considerable new powers, some worries obviously remain.

The threshold for the material to meet the definition of 'abhorrent violent material'

The eSafety commissioner has suggested that there is a 'very high threshold for material to meet the definition of AVM' (eSafety Commissioner, 2020). To agree with this statement would be to fail to acknowledge that, at least for terrorist act offences under the *Criminal Code* (Cth), the behavioural threshold for liability is not always set at a high level. Highly preparatory terrorist act offences exist in the *Code*, and, together with the definition of that form of AVC with the definition of the AVM, it could be said that the threshold for some recorded or streamed behaviour to satisfy the tests for AVM/AVC could likely be quite lower than asserted. Even the restrictions on who needs to produce the AVM under s. 474.31(1)(c), as set out above, could be thought to include such a significant number of potential persons that the threshold for defining online content as AVM should not be considered particularly high.

Proof of fault elements via responses to notices issued by the eSafety commissioner

Perhaps those at most risk of prosecution are not the corporations and major stakeholders with existing relationships of trust and consultation with the eSafety commissioner, but those small organisations and individuals who are suspected more easily of acting in bad faith. For those most vulnerable potential defendants of the failure to notify or remove offences, most troubling is how the required full subjective fault offences may be proved beyond reasonable doubt. Especially concerning is a twist on the required fault element proof that exists for the failure to remove offence in particular. As a result of s. 474.34(5), recklessness can be presumed merely by the objective facts that the eSafety commission has issued a notice about AVM (that a provider may not have received or understood) and that the access to the AVM can still be made following issuance of that notice. Subjective recklessness can therefore be proved by those objective facts alone rather than being proved beyond reasonable doubt on the standard subjective fault element tests as referred to above.

The eSafety commissioner's factsheet on these provisions supports our opinion that a controversial, evidentiary shortcut to proof of a subjective fault element exists and that there is some legal benefit in the commissioner issuing an AVM notice. Having issued a notice, recklessness as to failing to take down the material can be proved, not by examining the subjective mind of the individual or corporation who failed to remove or cease hosting AVM as per s 5.4 (1) or Part 2.5 of the *Criminal Code* (Cth), but merely as a presumption associated with the objective facts that the identified material has not been removed following the issuing of a notice:

> This [the issuing of a notice] is not a power to take down material. The notices do not require the AVM to be removed. However, if a service is later prosecuted for failing to remove or cease hosting AVM, the notice can be used in legal proceedings to show recklessness regarding the AVM. (eSafety Commissioner, 2020)

The ability to prove recklessness in this way seems to suggest that the drafters really wanted this offence to contain strict or absolute liability elements; however, the more controversial presumption mechanism was used to dilute the otherwise apparent requirements to prove full subjective fault. If there was a greater level of debate in parliament or in committee or via public consultation about these aspects of offence definition we wonder if it would have drawn more controversy.

Conclusion

The provisions introduced by the post-Christchurch Bill aimed at regulating the sharing of abhorrent violent material can be considered 'clumsy and flawed in many respects' and at least in two senses. Firstly, the hasty introduction of the Bill and its extremely short and under-deliberated passage through parliament suggests that there was limited time devoted to publicly debating these provisions.

This is particularly concerning when the nature and breadth of the powers and offences created by the Act are examined, despite reassurances from the eSafety commissioner herself. The way in which full subjective criminal liability is created by the Act, and fault elements of recklessness in the failure to remove offence in particular, can be proved via objective facts alone, and may mean that it is easy for some content service or hosting service providers to fall foul of the new offences, perhaps, especially if those providers are individuals or not large, well-known and informed corporations providing content or hosting services. In that and other contexts, these offences are controversial, and their extraterritorial reach and potential impact on international relations, if not international commerce, seemed to have warranted much more parliamentary debate than was afforded at the time (see also the discussion in Douek, 2020 p. 58).

The work of the eSafety commissioner as well as the discretion that may be exercised in favour of content service or hosting service providers by the Commonwealth director of public prosecutions will be interesting to monitor into the future. Any imbalance between a focus on prosecuting large, well-known corporations versus individuals under this new regime will be important to analyse, as will the relative use of failure to remove offences versus failure to notify offences. The financial and technical assistance required for some providers to even detect, if not also be able to remove, material that satisfies the complex legal definitions of AVM is something that the eSafety commissioner and the government of the day should consider. Any unintended consequences will be lamentable, and perhaps could have been preventable, in light of the haste and exceptionally thin deliberative processes used to pass such powerful provisions.

References

Belot, H. (2018, 28 November). Labor accuses government of tweaking parliament calendar to skip work and dodge scrutiny. *ABC News*. Retrieved from www.abc.net.au/news/2018-11-28/2019-parliamentary-sitting-calendar-called-surrender-document/10560474.

Blackbourn, J., McGarrity, N. & Roach, K. (2019). Understanding and responding to right wing terrorism. *Journal of Policing, Intelligence and Counter-Terrorism*, 14(3), 183–90. doi.org/10.1080/18335330.2019.1667014.

Carne, G. (2016). Sharpening the learning curve: Lessons from the Commonwealth Parliamentary Joint Committee of Intelligence and Security Review experience of five important aspects of terrorism laws. *University of Western Australia Law Review*, 41(1), 1–47.

Clough, J. (2007). Bridging the theoretical gap: The search for a realist model of corporate criminal liability. *Criminal Law Forum*, 18(3–4), 267–300. doi.org/10.1007/s10609-007-9040-y.

Clough, J. (2017). Improving the effectiveness of corporate criminal liability: Old challenges in a transnational world. In R. Levy, M. O'Brien, S. Rice, P. Ridge & Thornton, M. (Eds), *New Directions for Law in Australia: Essays in Contemporary Law Reform* (pp. 163–72) Canberra: ANU Press. doi.org/10.22459/ndla.09.2017.13.

Clough, J. & Mulhern, C. (2002). *The Prosecution of Corporations*. Melbourne: Oxford University Press.

Commonwealth. (2019a). *Parliamentary Debates*. House of Representatives, 4 April, pp. 1849–51 (Christian Porter, Attorney-General). Retrieved from parlinfo.aph.gov.au/parlInfo/download/chamber/hansardr/84457b57-5639-432a-b4df-68b704cb3563/toc_pdf/House%20of%20Representatives_2019_04_04_7041_Official.pdf;fileType=application%2Fpdf.

Commonwealth. (2019b). Explanatory Memorandum to the Criminal Code Amendment (Sharing of Abhorrent Violent Material) Bill 2019 (Cth). Retrieved from parlinfo.aph.gov.au/parlInfo/download/legislation/ems/s1201 _ems_08b22f92-a323-4512-bf31-bc55aab31a81/upload_pdf/19081em. pdf;fileType=application%2Fpdf.

Commonwealth. (2019c). *Parliamentary Debates.* House of Representatives, 4 April, pp. 1851–55 (Mark Dreyfus, Shadow Attorney-General). Retrieved from parlinfo.aph.gov.au/parlInfo/download/chamber/hansardr/84457b57- 5639-432a-b4df-68b704cb3563/toc_pdf/House%20of%20Representatives _2019_04_04_7041_Official.pdf;fileType=application%2Fpdf.

Commonwealth. (2019d). *Parliamentary Debates.* House of Representatives, 4 April, pp. 1855–57 (Adam Bandt). Retrieved from parlinfo.aph.gov.au/parlInfo/ download/chamber/hansardr/84457b57-5639-432a-b4df-68b704cb3563/ toc_pdf/House%20of%20Representatives_2019_04_04_7041_Official. pdf;fileType=application%2Fpdf.

Commonwealth. (2019e). *Parliamentary Debates.* House of Representatives, 4 April, pp. 1857–58 (Kerryn Phelps). Retrieved from parlinfo.aph.gov.au/parlInfo/ download/chamber/hansardr/84457b57-5639-432a-b4df-68b704cb3563/ toc_pdf/House%20of%20Representatives_2019_04_04_7041_Official. pdf;fileType=application%2Fpdf.

Commonwealth. (2019f). *Parliamentary Debates.* Senate, 3 April. Retrieved from parlinfo.aph.gov.au/parlInfo/download/chamber/hansards/e252d273-2978- 453f-86f5-ef9a8b66800f/toc_pdf/Senate_2019_04_03_7037_Official. pdf;fileType=application%2Fpdf.

Commonwealth. (2019g). *Parliamentary Debates.* House of Representatives, 4 April, pp. 1849–60. Retrieved from parlinfo.aph.gov.au/parlInfo/ download/chamber/hansardr/84457b57-5639-432a-b4df-68b704cb3563/ toc_pdf/House%20of%20Representatives_2019_04_04_7041_Official.pdf; fileType=application%2Fpdf.

Dalla-Pozza, D. (2010). *The Australian Approach to Enacting Counter-Terrorism Laws* [Unpublished doctoral dissertation]. University of New South Wales.

Dalla-Pozza, D. (2016). Refining the Australian counter-terrorism legislative framework: How deliberative has parliament been? *Public Law Review*, 27(4), 271–89.

Douek, E. (2020). Australia's 'abhorrent violent material' law: Shouting 'nerd harder' and drowning out speech. *Australian Law Journal*, 94, 41–60.

eSafety Commissioner. (2020). *Abhorrent Violent Material: Facts and Falsehoods.* Retrieved from www.esafety.gov.au/sites/default/files/2020-03/eSafety-AVM-factsheet.pdf.

Lynch, A. (2006) Legislating with urgency – the enactment of the *Anti-Terrorism Act (No 2) 2005. Melbourne University Law Review,* 30(3), 747–81.

Lynch, A., McGarrity, N & Williams, G. (2015). *Inside Australia's Anti-Terrorism Laws and Trials.* Sydney: NewSouth Publishing.

Moulds, S. (2018). Forum of choice? The legislative impact of the Parliamentary Joint Committee of Intelligence and Security. *Public Law Review,* 29(4), 287–94.

Muller, D. (2020). *The 2019 Federal Election.* Retrieved from parlinfo.aph.gov.au/parlInfo/download/library/prspub/7415275/upload_binary/7415275.pdf.

Parliament of Australia. (2019). *Sitting Calendar 2019 – Text Version.* Retrieved from www.aph.gov.au/About_Parliament/Sitting_Calendar/Sitting_calendar_2019-text_version.

Parliamentary Joint Committee on Law Enforcement. (2021). *Criminal Code Amendment (Sharing of Abhorrent Violent Material) Act 2019.* Retrieved from parlinfo.aph.gov.au/parlInfo/download/committees/reportjnt/024822/toc_pdf/CriminalCodeAmendment(SharingofAbhorrentViolentMaterial)Act2019.pdf;fileType=application%2Fpdf.

Parliamentary Joint Committee on Law Enforcement. (2022). *Criminal Code Amendment (Sharing of Abhorrent Violent Material) Act 2019 – Government Response.* Retrieved from www.aph.gov.au/Parliamentary_Business/Committees/Joint/Law_Enforcement/AVMAct/Government_Response.

Richardson, D. (2019). *Comprehensive Review of the Legal Framework of the National Intelligence Community Volume 4: Accountability and Transparency; Annexes.* Retrieved from www.ag.gov.au/system/files/2020-12/volume-4-accountability-and-transparency-annexes.PDF.

Uhr, J. (1998). *Deliberative Democracy in Australia.* Cambridge; Melbourne: Cambridge University Press.

7

Coarse and effect: Normalised anger online as an essential precondition to violence

Mark Kenny

Immediately upon commencing his three years as Australia's twenty-ninth prime minister, the nominally centre-right Malcolm Turnbull attempted to reframe the scourge of domestic violence by highlighting not merely the horrendous death toll[1] but its underlying sociocultural preconditions (Kenny, 2015). To his enduring credit, it became common to cite the wisdom of his spouse, Lucy Turnbull, who had noted persuasively that an undercurrent of misogyny was the soil from which acts of violence could spring. 'Let me say this to you: disrespecting women does not always result in violence against women. But all violence against women begins with disrespecting women', Turnbull told reporters while announcing new funding of $100 million to address the problem.

Founded anecdotally rather than empirically, the couple's favourite dictum allowed the prime minister to more powerfully enunciate the standard of language and personal deportment he expected from ministers and parliamentary members of his government. By extension, he sought further

---

1   The Australian Institute of Health and Welfare puts the number of fatal assaults by men of women at almost one a week, reporting that one woman was killed by a partner or former partner every nine days between 2014 and 2015 and 2015 and 2016.

to lift public awareness, particularly male awareness, of the corrosive downstream effects of an ostensibly harmless, normative culture of male preference and entitlement. Key to this was determinedly broadening the frame of endemic male-on-female violence so as to incorporate within its social conception underlying attitudes too often regarded as unrelated and ultimately, therefore, immaterial. This would include culturally normalised acts of discrimination from verbal slurs, sexist jokes and belittling behaviour, to physical threats and violent assault, the latter being invariably regarded as aberrant, freestanding and exceptional.

This chapter proceeds from the basis that Turnbull's observation need not be provable in an absolute or literal sense to be valuable. Its verisimilitude justifies its rhetorical deployment for transformative political purposes. That is, it not only rings true, but it usefully ties putatively harmless or merely *unenlightened* social conduct, particularly because it is normalised, with iterative degradations up to and including controlling behaviour, psychological torture and physical harm. Further, it will be argued that if disrespectful communications hitherto laughed off as 'harmless' can be so located on a relational continuum ending in violence against women, then, in all likelihood, a procedural link is plausible between the non-observance of civility in online discourse and the incidence of hate crimes – including gender-related violence – in the physical community.

In other words, a procedural relationship exists between (a) incivility, (b) cyber-hate and (c) physical violence, which, while not strictly causal, is, at a minimum, culturally contiguous and thus concomitant. And, further, that because the online community is potentially so vast – not limited by physical capacity constraints and the dictates of place – this concomitant relationship is anything but statistically unimportant. Indeed, even if the correlation between (a), (b) and (c) is relatively weak, the enormous scale, by way of the sheer number of malcontents reachable online and thus able to be radicalised, makes the security threat of a graduation from rage to intimidation and then to violence, numerically significant. Previous chapters in this book have outlined the important role played by online, alt-right communities in the Christchurch terrorist attack. Here, the widespread normalisation of incivility and hate speech within online communities is examined in more depth.

Among the things this chapter does not set out to do is advocate new laws governing online presentations that would inhibit reasoned debate, proscribe anger per se, ban profanity or even see digital companies act of their own volition to deplatform users merely for exhibiting too much passion, poor social graces or for taking unpopular policy positions. While that case can be made, it is a separate field of discussion and raises legitimate concerns over the freedom of the internet, and fundamental questions regarding freedom of expression. Rather, it will be suggested (albeit warily) that just as it was (and is) accepted in pre-internet society that there are agreed forms of social interaction, and that breaches will bring costs from rebuke to social exclusion, such mores could be more consistently applied online by those with notional leadership positions.

In short, socially responsible users of platforms like Twitter could (and should) exercise restraint personally and no matter what the provocation, apply the same standards to their own interactions that they would automatically observe in their face-to-face communications. And they should simply cease to correspond with those who blithely dispense with such civilities, whether through the issuing of physical and sexualised threats, vile and abusive language, wilful lies or discriminatory statements.

Two different standards of exchange

Too often, Twitter exchanges proceed past the point of civilised difference or simple information sharing and descend into name calling and bilateral vitriol. This 'dys-coarse' (dysfunctional discourse) need not be one-sided or restricted to anonymous or unknown individuals with an axe to grind. Examples abound of prominent *Twitterati* – journalists, broadcasters, actors and others occupying positions of some social vantage and with large profiles (or followings) – engaging in and thus normalising aggressive/reactive behaviour, behaviour that most such persons would not dream of undertaking during chance conversations in the street, or at the local supermarket or sportsground.

Why does this matter? Because journalists, academics, artists and entertainers wield significant popular capital. That is, they tend to have vastly more reach and standard-setting leadership on social media platforms than do regular individuals. In this regard they are also the links or common points between disparate and otherwise disaggregated agitators who, through deliberate provocation and response-seeking, manage to leverage their online reach.

In 2016, Antoci et al. analysed what they called 'the dynamics of civil and uncivil ways of interaction in online social networks and their consequences for collective welfare'. They concluded, inter alia, that incivility, including hate speech, false information, harassment and other antisocial behavioural forms, was growing on social networking sites (SNS), while also sounding a hopeful note:

> Agents can choose to interact with others – politely or rudely – in SNS, or to opt out from online social networks to protect themselves from incivility. We find that, when the initial share of the population of polite users reaches a critical level, civility becomes generalized if its payoff increases more than that of incivility with the spreading of politeness in online interactions. (Antoci et al., 2016, p. 1)

For prominent public figures, *how* they go about their online interactions may be as influential – and thus norm-reinforcing – as what they say. If all such high-profile people eschewed vulgarity (except perhaps for the occasional comic effect) and adopted the policy of blocking or muting any interlocutor who crossed the line into abuse, it would not take long for an improved standard to take hold (Antoci et al., 2016). Twitter, for example, offers the ability to *block* or *mute* other users; the former notifies the offender that they have been removed from the recipient's comment feed and the latter removes an unwanted user without notifying the offender. Denied vicarious access entry to the larger followings of celebrities, contributors given to provocative, exaggerated and hateful discourse may quickly find themselves shouting to diminishing audiences.

Opting out of SNS has been the course of action of several prominent figures in Australian politics. One of them, the Labor frontbencher Ed Husic, abandoned Twitter in September 2017, forsaking a large and politically useful following. A year later he explained that the site rewarded divisiveness and aggression:

> What gets you a lot of attention is how much you stand out from the last person's epic sledge. We should ask: is social media acting like an accelerant in an overheated, divisive atmosphere in politics? (Husic, 2018)

Another who opted out was the prominent conservative journalist and commentator Chris Kenny (the author's cousin), who had become a magnet for left-wing attacks on Twitter.

The town square

Social media platforms like Facebook and Twitter are often compared to a town square with the aim of lauding their pure, untrammelled democratic and participatory bona fides. It is an immediately attractive idea – particularly within aging democracies succumbing to the now well-recognised signs of institutional fatigue, from declining trust in traditional politics to impatience over political gridlock. Through this frame of reference, parliamentary representation is in practice viewed as an elite and even anachronistic province: restrictive, exclusive, self-interested and, very often, corrupt. And journalists, along with their corporate/establishment employers, are routinely positioned as part of the same privileged ecosystem.

The World Wide Web is different. Advocates celebrate this unedited, non-curated space in which all comers get a voice, irrespective of education level, wealth, political allegiance or opinion. But how good is the village square analogy, really? At their best, the social media 'disrupters' – Facebook, Google, Twitter et al. – have been forces for justice, enabling women and other disempowered groups to connect and organise, facilitating resistance to autocratic regimes such as in the Arab Spring Uprising in 2010–11 or the Hong Kong protests in 2019–20. Social media platforms have been instrumental in exposing corruption and pursuing justice for the disadvantaged (Marantz, 2019, p. 3). As discussed by Leitch above, the final report of ACCC's digital platforms inquiry noted that there have been many benefits for individuals and groups, but significant concerns have arisen also in relation to market power, disinformation and 'harmful content'. The widespread disintermediation of the information flow brought about by the digital era has shocked the sclerotic institutional machinery of post-industrial societies, bringing powerful interests to new account and dismantling longstanding protections around access to information.

Politicians have read the rage and responded in various ways, from embracing greater openness to ideas and myriad opportunities for community input, broadly describable as democratic rejuvenation, to rank populism and democratic diminution. The former is designed to reinvigorate representation and improve democratic function, while the latter is calculated to capitalise on the electoral dividends available in stoking divisions and ratcheting up community resentment.

Donald Trump, unquestionably the most spectacular and effective Twitter politician yet seen, was one aspiring political leader who quickly understood how to harness the web's populist potential. Trump demonstrated that the World Wide Web is a demagogue's dream, offering real-time communication en masse, ideal for emotional messaging and perfect for the weaponisation of inchoate rage. Elsewhere, I have characterised populism as hyper-democracy, but another useful critique comes from the British writer Martin Amis and his 2020 novel, *Inside Story*, in which he describes it as 'a kind of Counter-Enlightenment' exemplified by Trump's comment after his surprise 2016 victory: 'I love the poorly-educated, we're the smartest people, we're the most loyal people'.

Trump's use of the microblog to speak directly with ordinary voters, bypassing even his own advisers and officials, short-circuited mainstream politics, stripping it of much of its time-worn artifice. Voters – and online citizens across the globe – gained direct and often instantaneous access to the president's most unguarded reactions, providing a window to his eponymous administration's avowedly anti-intellectual tabloid iconoclasm. To many political 'outsiders', this conveyed a powerful air of authenticity and ownership, of undiluted bottom-to-top representation.

Central to this new relationship was Trump's demonisation of traditional media, which he successfully portrayed as rent with lies, beholden to special interests, captive to elite sensibility and unpatriotically cosmopolitan. But division is an inherently small project and his administration's preference for political manipulation over policy rigour was laid cruelly bare amid the catastrophic onset of the COVID-19 pandemic. By election day, 2 November 2020, his populist push had flamed out its subterranean peat-fire of resentment, unable to match the more restorative above-ground promise of the Democrat contender, Joe Biden. A populist disrupter to the bitter end, Trump's final climax would come two months later when, on 6 January 2021, the defeated president's ferocious anger licensed his supporters to storm the Capitol to stop the official declaration of Biden as the winner. So fundamental was this challenge to the world's most powerful democracy, that finally the platforms Twitter and Facebook suspended Trump's accounts. Twitter did so two days after the Capitol siege, permanently suspending the president's account while noting specifically how his tweets were 'being received and interpreted on and off Twitter' and the risk of 'further incitement of violence'. Facebook also suspended Trump's account and, at the time of writing, its internal review process had endorsed that suspension until 2023.

Trump's extraordinary rise owed much to the lawless frontier ethics of the internet, with the president eschewing the usual filters and systems to establish a volatile, if popular movement that took him to the White House and came very close to keeping him there. Even in falling short of victory, Trump secured 74,216,154 votes nationally, which is more than any previous presidential candidate, including all those who won. Biden, however, received even more, at 81,268,924. In any event, Biden easily surpassed the required 270 Electoral College votes, finishing with 306 to Trump's 232.

It was an administration tailored for the internet age. Trump did not even pretend to govern for the nation, or build consensus across the political aisle. Rather, like the hate merchants of social networking sites, his project was about ratcheting up ever more fervour among those voters already in his camp. By its nature, the disintermediation offered by social media 'platforms' and capitalised on by Trump is post-institutional, proving that, as with all metaphors, the digital town square has its limits. These limits are discussed in more depth in the following chapter.

A real civic space would not be so poorly lit that speakers would not be visible or identified. Anonymity is a prevalent feature of online presence and appears to be availed disproportionately by those seeking to harass, intimidate and silence. Neither would a real town square stay peaceful for long if the people gathered together in a face-to-face situation, adopted the modes of abusive behaviour common and normalised online. Which is to say, the debasement of longstanding social mores observable in the flippant recourse to profanity, deliberate trolling, *argumentum ad hominem* and a rudeness uninhibited by the personal accountabilities attaching to non-digital communication, do not sit well within the town square analogue.

The standard response to such complaints is dismissive: *people swear and make hollow threats, but it doesn't mean anything really. This is what genuinely free and robust exchange looks like.* Thus, we are counselled to *harden up!* But why is aggression online given this leave pass, this special dispensation to insult and threaten as if somehow uniquely, in cyberspace, no material harm can accrue, no responsibility need be taken?

While much online incivility is widely considered freestanding and harmless, it might also be viewed as the point of origin for actions of a more physically intimidatory and divisive nature. Or, to adapt Turnbull's words, not all trolling, racism, religious bigotry, misogyny, defamation, character assassination and verbal abuse result in explosive violence – like the Christchurch massacre – but all such violence begins in these moral badlands.

Moreover, when the wellsprings of such social negatives are tolerated and normalised, and where complainants are derided as 'snowflakes' for their 'over-sensitivity', a step has been taken away from normative restraints that reinforce respectful boundaries, and towards something else. Indeed, when abuse is laughed off as mere robustness, are we not placing a heavier social sanction on the complainant than the offender? It is as if the act of objecting to trolling, sexism and other vilification is viewed as more threatening to online discourse than these destructive forms.

Trolling alone: From malcontent to mal-intent

Anecdotally, the relationship between hate speech and dangerous escalations motivated by that hatred is uncontroversial. Indeed, such an outcome is explicitly the point. Less settled is the link between incivility and hateful rhetoric. Equally unclear is why incivility apologists are so sure that the deterioration of social interchange has no negative sequelae offline, especially as the practitioners of anger are so frank on this point. Right-wing culture warriors have even been open about the formative radicalising role of hateful rhetoric.

New Yorker writer Andrew Marantz quotes one such self-declared extremist – an actual murderer – charting his own journey from orthodox right-wing libertarianism to violent racism (Marantz, 2019). As Marantz notes, two weeks before using three handguns and an assault rifle in a Pittsburgh synagogue in 2018 to gun down the faithful, the shooter had reposted a stick figure cartoon specifically detailing what adherents openly refer to as the 'libertarian-to-far-right-pipeline'. Within extreme right circles, this pipeline is the mechanism by which cyber-rants can be used to deliver staged epiphanies helping inductees to progress in increments of outrage from right-leaning misanthropes to the roiling vengeance mentality typical of far-right extremism.

A crucial element for attracting and recruiting is relatability, the illusion of some measure of normality. In his book *Fascists Among Us: Online Hate and the Christchurch Massacre*, Sparrow (2019) cites mainstream media interviews in Australia with known fascists and neo-Nazis in 2016, including the erstwhile United Patriots Front's leader, Blair Cottrell, as instrumental in this regard. A self-declared fan of Adolf Hitler, Cottrell was again hosted in 2018 on Sky News Australia by a former mainstream conservative politician, one-time Northern Territory Chief Minister Adam Giles. That interview (the fact of it and its abhorrent content), provoked a reaction within the subscription broadcaster itself and beyond with the then-Race Discrimination Commissioner Tim Soutphommasane (2018) warning Australian media of the consequences of such normalisation via Twitter that:

> We've come not to expect much from the nocturnal programming at @SkyNewsAust – but featuring a neo-Nazi with a history of crime and violence is a shameful low. It also highlights how extremists are being dangerously accommodated by sections of the Australian media.

The mainstreaming of extreme political fanaticism such as the airing of Cottrell's toxic agenda has twin effects. From his point of view, both are good. First, it directly reaches a small but potentially like-minded audience who are buoyed by the publicity, encouraged by their progress, and (no doubt) further impressed by their leader's perspicacity, courage and media prowess. Second, it has the concomitant effect of de-thorning marginally less extreme right-wing views on race, religion, feminism and white supremacy, rendering them comparatively reasonable. A pointer to this is the clear condemnation of Cottrell's views across the political and media spectrum, while other embedded commentators proffering similar, but less severe opinions, pass unremarked (Sparrow, 2019).

'Sky after dark', as it is known even by working journalists at the broadcaster, provides a line-up of hardline conservatives peddling resentment politics and railing against the inchoate left-wing bias of just about everything.

133

With some worthy exceptions, and with some differences issue-by-issue, hosts generally propagate extreme right-wing precepts on immigration, climate change, vaccines and, of course, the perceived death of free speech. Falsehoods abound. Denis Muller (2021) recently listed several:

> Rowan Dean's and Alan Jones's repeated ravings about the 'stolen' US election; Peta Credlin's false claim that [Kevin] Rudd's petition for a Murdoch royal commission was an exercise in data-harvesting, for which she had to apologise as part of a confidential defamation settlement; Jones's disinformation about mask-wearing; James Morrow calling the Trump impeachment trial a 'sinister plot by Democrats against the American people'.

Provocative lies and exaggerations are the lingua franca of the rancorous right.

As Leitch notes elsewhere in these pages, a decision was taken in the immediate aftermath of the Christchurch attacks by the Aotearoa New Zealand Prime Minister Jacinda Ardern, backed by multiple other parties including mainstream media organisations, to deny the shooter a name and thus any sense of personal notoriety. Yet against the undercurrent of more mainstream validation of right-wing grievance (as distinct from support for the terrorist atrocity itself), denial of the shooter's humanity may achieve little.

Sparrow (2019) concludes that a well-intentioned aim of avoiding amplification of the shooter's message missed the object of his plan, which was to narrow-cast to and inspire a predetermined 'online audience'. Moreover, limiting public discussion and scrutiny of same helped to obscure the extent to which his manifesto drew on extant strands of populism, racism and conservatism. He surmises that:

> A refusal to discuss Person X's ideas meant in practice, a refusal to acknowledge how many of them were widely shared in the mainstream, including by major outlets. You did not need to search the dark web to find examples of Islamophobia; you could encounter anti-immigrant rhetoric on every TV station and in every tabloid as well as in the statements of major politicians. (Sparrow, 2019, p. 119)

Validation

Crucially, tolerance of threatening and directly abusive language and actions is not limited to right-wing discourse. Aggression has been normalised and implicitly validated by a corresponding left-wing anger, providing extremists of either stripe with what Sparrow (2019) has characterised as 'cover' within the noise. Conservative Liberal MP Nicolle Flint announced her intention to retire from federal politics at the next election, citing accumulated trauma from a vicious, highly personalised and 'coordinated sexist campaign', much of it online. She named left-aligned members and supporters of trade unions and the progressive activist group Get Up! for the abuse, declaring it left her traumatised:

> I ask the Leader of the Opposition, where was he and where was his predecessor and where were the senior Labor women when GetUp, Labor, and union supporters chased, harassed and screamed at me everywhere I went in the lead-up to the 2019 election? (McCulloch, 2021)

She labelled the campaign, which also saw her office defaced with words 'prostitute' and 'skank', as 'horrendous, sexist and misogynist abuse'.

In addition, several high-profile Australian public figures of a progressive disposition are known for their abrasive presentations online, presentations that include swearing, impugning the motives and intelligence of interlocutors, and generally displaying abusive and dismissive characteristics that would be unthinkable in direct person-to-person exchanges or in their professional capacities. While, in many cases, one might be tempted to agree with such sentiments, deeper questions of systemic harm arise. That web fundamentalists generally struggle with this concept is as surprising as their arguments are unpersuasive.

Consider this illustration: imagine two numerically similar societies, one in which social norms of basic civility, manners and a sense of proportion guide disagreements, and another one in which no such guard rails exist, where disagreements freely escalate from bitter resentment to abuse and physical threats. Of the two, which would be the more volatile, proto-violent society? This is why every successful community has developed norms of behaviour that set out expectations of how individuals should reasonably conduct themselves. Such social strictures are, of course, never universally observed, and are themselves politically neutral. Doubtless, they have provided stability and enhanced personal security by cementing a status quo in which the few retain their advantage at the expense of the many. Yet throughout human history such systems have arisen and the durable ones have even proved capable of renewal and reform.

Parliamentary representation is one formalised system that exhibits this combination of rigidity: highly codified expressive forms allowing conflict mediation within time-honoured and repeatedly enforced norms. But there is also a modicum of flexibility granting the latitude required to accommodate new interests and the inevitable undulations of human emotion and subjectivity.

In adversarial Westminster parliaments such as those of Britain and its former colonies, green-carpeted, lower house chambers feature red lines running along in front of each of the two front benches. 'Members may speak only from where they were called, which must be within the House [of Commons]', Westminster's parliamentary website explains. 'They may not speak from the floor of the House between the red lines (traditionally supposed to be two sword-lengths apart).' Arcane and ceremonial, this dates back to the earliest parliaments when members (exclusively men) could be armed, disagreements threatened to become physical and a degree of separation was considered prudent. Its policing role now is not literal but normative. It reminds MPs why parliament was first created, and why disagreement is to be contained within behavioural boundaries consistent with even temper, and institutional survival.

Functionally similar principles govern competition in other fields from literature to the academy to sporting codes. Implicit in each is the working acknowledgement that systemic value is always superior to the suasion of any one set of interests, no matter how passionately held. Interest mediation in the digital sphere, though, knows no such bounds. Attempts to moderate social behaviour in the digital realm elicit immediate and ferocious objection, usually in defence of free speech, and against censoriousness.

Circling back to the two societies illustrated above, it becomes clear that the problem is that the system in a cyber sense – the agreed forum for disagreement – has no intrinsic value attributed to it and plays no constraining role. In the internet age, replete with its supranational social media giants, the two social systems coexist: the socially regulated physical world, and the defiantly unregulated frontier of cyberspace.

Yet they are hardly separate. The same actors operate within both spheres, the legally regulated and socially codified real world, and the laissez faire online community where anonymity, deliberate misinformation, physical disembodiment and contempt for social mores mean that anything goes.

The internet, then, is post-institutional: extra-jurisdictional. An ungoverned expanse where spectacular lies compete for space with more mundane truths and excess begets excess. Even the big players, Facebook, Google, Twitter, Snapchat, insist that they are mere platforms rather than publishers. Twitter, until recently Donald Trump's medium of maximum effect, is notorious for what the author has called elsewhere its 'brave soldiers of anonymity' – legions of users cowering behind fake names and joke photographs, an assortment of bots, trolls and digital ne'er-do-wells. Unbound by such personal restraints as would apply in physical interactions, these people are free to parade their partisan rage against any and all who do not assertively promote their extreme position.

Public figures are subject to aggressive personal insults, foul language and, in the case of journalists – especially loathed on the left and the right for not taking a position at all – extraordinary claims of unprofessional bias. Once again, women suffer the most aggressive treatment, often laced with foul language either suggestive of or explicitly threatening direct sexual assault. What follows is one such example, but journalists, particularly women journalists, have all experienced and received such outrageous, unsolicited feedback. Respected Sky News Australia journalist Laura Jayes posted a sample in March of the vulgar abuse directed to her on Twitter: 'You f*cking idiot c*nt. Your [sic] a disgrace … you are [sic] complete f*ck wit and flop of a journalist' (Jayes, 18–19 March 2021). The temptation to respond in a similarly aggressive tone is strong. Yet this can be worse than pointless because, for the original offender, such retorts constitute both a vindication of grievance and a validation of their abandonment of civility. Moreover, responding in any form lends the cloak of normality to a mode of exchange that has, as one of its natural progressions, the sharpening of grievance, the deepening of rage and thus a greater propensity to violence.

Terror nullius

The debate about whether social media has generated abuse, or merely laid bare an undercurrent of resentment that was always there, will no doubt continue. But, in one sense, it misses a crucial and observable fact: digital disinhibition has had the effect of normalising the expression of anger and aggression, the articulation of which would have been seen as aberrant in pre-digital times. The effect has been to turn such antisocial behaviour into a less illegitimate, increasingly mainstream frame of public discussion.

One danger is that, for those growing up with the World Wide Web, uncivil social exchange could come to feel passé. For these individuals, the virtual world may already be the dominant mode of social interaction, meaning its relative, or resting, level of incivility becomes the new normal. That said, it is certainly true that the digital age neither created verbal aggression nor pioneered its rapid substitution for sophisticated argument.

Public figures have always been attacked. Charles Darwin, for example, experienced abuse when he published *The Descent of Man, and Selection in Relation to Sex* in 1871. In a piece marking the book's 150th anniversary, Hesketh and Meiring (2021) referenced this harsh reality:

> Leading feminist Frances Power Cobbe rejected Darwin's theory of morality as 'simious' [having ape-like qualities] while *The Times* thundered Darwin's ideas could encourage 'the most murderous revolutions'. Darwin also received hate mail from offended readers like Mr. D. Thomas, who referred to him as a 'venerable old Ape'. Darwin began to be regularly caricatured as an ape in the press.

Typically, these *argumentum ad hominem* were poorly thought through. Indeed, it was the groundbreaking scientist's very own contention that humans were closely related to primates, and, moreover, that such animals exhibited nobility, aesthetic preference and even moral substance. In the final observation of the book, Darwin confessed he would rather be related to a 'heroic little monkey' than to a 'savage who delights to torture his enemies' (Hesketh and Meiring, 2021).

Conclusion

The proposition at the heart of this chapter is that a generalised social indifference to vituperative online discourse, as if it has no bleed-back implications for non-digital behaviour, helps to normalise aggression. And, in so doing, it also engenders coarse demagogues such as Trump, for whom personal abuse and derision become an acceptable and effective rallying tool.

Inadvertently, liberal insouciance to incivility may license more severe dysfunctions, specifically by desensitising the broader population – online and off – to the menacing lexicons of misogyny and, therefore, domestic and sexual violence, and racial epithets, from which racial hate crimes arise. It may also enable extremist ideologies to propagate support for real-world terrorist attacks such as Christchurch. It is not necessary to definitively link deliberate online harm to violence in a causal sense, but rather to observe that it is an essential and concomitant precondition.

Criticism of widespread incivility online invariably invites straw man responses alleging fetters on freedom of speech. This rights-based argument has obvious populist appeal because, in common with all populist messaging, it is simple. It is also simply wrong. The right to free expression is already attenuated in multiple ways from cultural norms to defamation laws, and national security concerns. In complex, pluralist societies it carries with it the responsibility of restraint. A corollary is that the absence of vituperation from an individual's public discussions is itself a recognition of the existence of alternative perspectives and communal commitment.

The unstated aim of civil society is its own perpetuation. While there are legitimate critiques of the way power and privilege have been shielded from the morally righteous imperatives of social justice and economic equality under this respectable guise, progress has been possible. Technological leaps since the advent of the printing press have both exacerbated and then ameliorated disadvantage. The internet is one such technology. But its capacity to be used by populists and their divisive agents for social disintegration, violent antisocial discourse and personal intimidation is an obvious danger.

The promotion and reinforcement of an online discourse closer to the mores pertaining to offline society could ensure that this vast meta-democratic communications revolution represents a leap forward, rather than a leap into the dark.

References

Amis, M. (2020). *Inside Story: A Novel*. London: Jonathan Cape.

Antoci, A., Delfino, A., Paglieri, F., Panebianco, F. & Sabatini, F. (2016). Civility vs. incivility in online social interactions: An evolutionary approach. *PLoS ONE*, 11. doi.org/10.1371/journal.pone.0164286.

Bates, L. (2020). *Men Who Hate Women: From Incels to Pickup Artists, the Truth about Extreme Misogyny and How it Affects Us All*. London: Simon and Schuster.

Chaudhry, I. & Gruzd, A. (2019). Expressing and challenging racist discourse on Facebook: How social media weaken the 'spiral of silence' theory. *Policy & Internet: Early View*. doi.org/10.1002/poi3.197.

Dexter, R. (2021, 17 March). 'Stalking and threats': PM says campaign against Nicolle Flint was one of the ugliest he's seen. *Sydney Morning Herald*. Retrieved from www.smh.com.au/national/albanese-concedes-poor-treatment-of-female-liberal-mp-by-labor-20210317-p57bdn.html.

Doherty, B. (2020, 24 February). ASIO boss warns of rising foreign interference and far-right extremism in Australia. *Guardian*, Australia. Retrieved from www.theguardian.com/australia-news/2020/feb/24/rightwing-extremism-a-real-and-growing-threat-asio-chief-says-in-annual-assessment.

Duggan, M. (2017). Online harassment. *Pew Research Center, Internet and Technology*. Retrieved from www.pewresearch.org/internet/2017/07/11/online-harassment-2017/.

Gorman, G. (2019). *Troll Hunting: Inside the World of Online Hate and its Human Fallout*. Melbourne: Hardie Grant.

Hesketh, I. & Meiring, H. J. (2021, 25 February). Guide to the classics: Darwin's *The Descent of Man* 150 years on – sex, race and our 'lowly' ape ancestry. *Conversation*. theconversation.com/guide-to-the-classics-darwins-the-descent-of-man-150-years-on-sex-race-and-our-lowly-ape-ancestry-155305.

Husic, E. (2018, 18 September). 'Hi. I'm Ed. I'm an MP. It's been 12 months since my last tweet.' *Sydney Morning Herald* 'op-ed'. Retrieved from www.smh.com.au/politics/federal/hi-i-m-ed-i-m-an-mp-it-s-been-12-months-since-my-last-tweet-20180917-p5047q.html.

Jayes, L. (2021, 18–19 March). Twitter. (Series of 'tweets' dealing with online abuse and threats to journalists and politicians). Retrieved from twitter.com/ljayes.

Kenny, M. (2015, 22 September). Prime Minister Malcolm Turnbull to go hard against domestic violence. *Sydney Morning Herald*. Retrieved from www.smh.com.au/politics/federal/malcolm-turnbull-to-go-hard-against-domestic-violence-20150923-gjtcui.html.

Marantz, A. (2019). *Antisocial: How Online Extremists Broke America*. New York: Viking.

McCulloch, D. (2021, 17 March). Liberal delivers emotional speech on women. *Canberra Times*. Retrieved from www.canberratimes.com.au/story/7170402/liberal-delivers-emotional-speech-on-women/.

Muller, D. (2021, 22 February). Is Sky News shifting Australian politics to the right? Not yet, but there is cause for alarm. *Conversation*. Retrieved from theconversation.com/is-sky-news-shifting-australian-politics-to-the-right-not-yet-but-there-is-cause-for-alarm-155356.

Soutphommasane, T. (2018, 5 August). @timsout, 1.46 am. Twitter.com.

Sparrow, J. (2019). *Fascists Among Us: Online Hate and the Christchurch Massacre*. Brunswick, Victoria: Scribe.

Twitter Inc. (2021, 8 January). Permanent suspension of @realDonaldTrump. Twitter Official Blog. Retrieved from blog.twitter.com/en_us/topics/company/2020/suspension.html.

8

Performances of power – the site of public debate

Katrina Grant

In 2009, the protests against the election result in Iran began to play out not just on the streets of the capital Tehran but online. Shortly after the protests, Lev Grossman wrote in *Time* magazine that Twitter (at that point the platform was only three years old) was 'ideal for a mass protest movement, both very easy for the average citizen to use and very hard for any central authority to control' (Grossman, 2009). Over 10 years later, the latter seems to have remained true, but the idea that it is serving the 'average citizen' is now less convincing. The potential for online social media platforms like Twitter, Facebook, Reddit and others to be subject to manipulation and used for the spread of misinformation and abuse has been in the spotlight in recent years (Geeng et al., 2020). The hope (perhaps always naive) that online platforms would give a voice and a presence to millions of citizens and drive positive democratic change has not really come to pass. Although there are movements that have used the online space to provide visibility for traditionally invisible and marginalised groups in mainstream media (such as #metoo and #blacklivesmatter), there is the flip side of online spaces used to drive coordinated programs of abuse against women (#gamergate), to inflame hatred of religious minorities, and the use of bots to disseminate misinformation and offer counternarratives (Massanari, 2017; Cadwalladr, 2017). Social media has also become a public stage for the performance of power and, in extreme cases, violent acts (Irwin-Rogers and Pinkney, 2017). The prominent role of social media in the 2019 terrorist attack in Christchurch, which was livestreamed on Facebook, has added further weight to calls to regulate online space.

As a historian, there is always a temptation to look for parallels between current trends and those of the past. The new world ushered in by digital connectivity can be compared to other moments when technology transformed communication: the telegraph, when steam allowed faster travel. The purpose of this chapter is to look specifically at how places designed and built for public debate have enabled the performance of power and social hierarchies by certain groups in society. The intention is both to show continuities and to point out distinct differences. This chapter aims to add some depth and background to the comparisons between online spaces of debate, like Twitter, Facebook and other online forums with the public squares, speakers' corners and private spaces of the past that allowed the dissemination of ideas and supported propaganda and reinforcing social hierarchies that benefit some while discriminating against others.

This idea, that a 'space' designed for publics to gather in could be used to reshape society, to give voice to the populace, and offer a challenge to, or a check upon, power, is not new. In the following chapter by Nurmikko-Fuller and Pickering, the long history of public debates about and political responses to the advent of new communication technologies is examined. Here the focus is on digital technology as a public space. For millennia the design of towns and cities has deliberately included, or excluded, types of open, public spaces designed to support the functioning of that society. These places, whether designed as town squares, agora or piazzas, were intended to provide space for gatherings of people to come together to voice opinion and debate, to vote and to be given access and insight into the politics that governed their daily lives. These physical places have performed a role as stages for the symbolic and real enactment of political power, regardless of whether this is the power of a populace as in democracy, an individual (absolutism) or even a religious elite (theocracy). Online social media sites, like Twitter, Facebook, Reddit, etc., are often compared to public squares (Kavanaugh et al., 2010; Mascaro and Goggins, 2012); but, do they share characteristics with the Ancient Greek agora or the twentieth-century civic plaza? This chapter will examine why public space is important in the performance of political power and its links with democracy, governance and ideals of civil society through several case studies. It will also examine not just the reality of these urban spaces, but the idea of them, and how the symbolic ideal of the 'city square' has come to inform our understanding, use and regulation of online social platforms (Hamilton, 2021).

The Arab Spring and Twitter as a site of protest

The Iranian protests and then the Arab Spring, which saw uprisings against governments across countries in the Middle East, was one of the first times that social media – blogging, Twitter and Facebook – began to be seen as something other than a purely 'social' network or type of media platform (West, 2009; El-Nawawy and Khamis, 2012). The mainstream media, and by extension broader society, began to regard social platforms as something more than just useful tools for connecting with friends. Social media began to be talked about as a site for protest and dissent. It was described as a place analogous to the streets of Tehran or Tahrir Square in Cairo.

Heidi Campbell and Diana Hawk analysed the ways in which Al Jazeera described the use of social media during the Arab Spring and they report that social media was frequently described not just as a news medium but as 'a site itself' (Campbell and Hawk, 2012). They quote a report from the Qatari news outlet from February 2011 that described 'the battle in Egypt fought on the pages of Elvis Bok [Facebook]' (Campbell and Hawk, 2012). Specific Facebook sites set up to protest police brutality were described as 'rallying points' (BBC, 2011; El-Nawawy and Khamis, 2012). Social media users were also described as 'online citizens' or 'netizens', a use of language usually applied to people who share residence in a physical place, a city, region or country (El-Nawawy and Khamis, 2012). Also of significance, and discussed at the time, was the default public nature of Twitter, which set it apart from other social media such as Facebook. Grossman in *Time* described it as follows: 'e-mail and Facebook ... those media aren't public. They don't broadcast, as Twitter does' (Grossman, 2009). This created an identity for Twitter in particular as the new public square, accessible by anyone and designed to facilitate open discussion.

Quite soon after the protest movements had finished, or at least faded from daily global reporting, a more critical discussion began to take place. The role of social media was questioned: was it exaggerated by the Western journalists? Were the 'real-time' updates, pictures and videos put on Twitter specifically for a global audience, rather than those on the ground? Evgeny Morozov critiqued the Western media's breathless excitement over the power of social media to unseat authoritarian governments. He wrote: 'Whether technology was actually driving the protests remains a big unknown. It is certainly a theory that many in the West find endearing' (Morozov, 2009). A report from 2012 observed that Twitter participation inside Iran at the time was actually quite low, with only '8500 Twitter users who self-reported as Iranian in May 2009 … [and] less than 1000 of those were active during the election period' (Aday et al., 2010). What this report concluded, however, was that Twitter and other online media platforms mattered because they became the main source of information about what was happening on the ground. The new platforms circumvented the restrictions placed on journalists and that meant that 'the outside world's perceptions of the protests were crucially shaped by Twitter (as conveyed through blogs and other means), amateur videos uploaded to YouTube and Facebook, and other sources' (Aday et al., 2010). Even while the protests themselves unfolded in real space, Twitter and Facebook became sites where these social movements were opened up to larger publics who were not necessarily physically located in the cities themselves.

This ideal of the city public space and its link to democracy has a long history; the Ancient Greek and early modern Italian city states attained an iconic status as symbols of the connection between urban design and politics (Low, 2009). Designers who laid or replanned cities in the nineteenth and twentieth centuries privileged civic spaces as symbols of democracy, though often with mixed success in terms of their actual use. In the twenty-first century the rise of online spaces like Twitter and Facebook have offered an alternative gathering place for citizens, yet the city itself retains both a symbolic and real importance as a driver for civic engagement and the preservation of democratic government. Both online and offline spaces remain important for real and symbolic performances of power by the populace, and both are susceptible to manipulation by individuals or groups who wish to manipulate public opinion and reshape political power structures.

The case of ancient Greece and Rome

The origins of the idea of an urban space for public debate as a key part of democracy, or at least egalitarian politics, are strongly linked to places like the Agora of Athens in ancient Greece and the Forum Romanum in ancient Rome. These spaces have come to represent an ideal of a public space that enabled, and even encouraged, democracy, free speech and allowed the populace, or *polis*, to access and scrutinise political representatives and leaders. The name agora means 'to meet' and also 'to speak publicly', 'place of assembly', 'to proclaim', 'to harangue' and so on (Liddell and Scott, 1940). This demonstrates the extent to which the place itself was aligned with the act of speaking publicly at the time. Of course, it was not necessarily a space of free speech for all. In ancient Greece, the agora 'was the property of male citizens' (Rotroff and Lamberton, 2006), meaning that slaves and women were excluded (although the reality, as explained by Rotroff and Lamberton, was more complex). On the other hand, Athens distinguished itself by including the poor in this space, by offering them pay that allowed them to attend the assembly and therefore offered them a level of equality in terms of public speech (Bejan, 2017).

What is of interest in this essay is not so much the reality of the agora in ancient Greece, but the idea of it, both at the time – in the writings that have survived – and in the millennia since the agora has been presented as a place that allows free, public speech; and that this ability to speak and debate publicly in turn supports a democratic society (Urbinati, 2002; Saxonhouse, 2005; Arendt, 2019). In other words, without this particular urban space, the society itself would have been different. The development of cities is often linked to the development of civilised society (at least in the Western tradition). The shift to living in a city transformed the laws and actions that governed life from individualistic, concerned only with one's own family group, to public (Frampton, 2017). At the heart of these early city states, like Athens, was the agora, a place deliberately designed and denoted as one in which the ideals of the society would be practised in public. The reasons for the success of the Greek city states are obviously complex, but the *idea* of the agora as either instrumental in its success, or as a material realisation of it values, is powerful. Saul Frampton has asked 'was the rise of the polis somehow the astonishing aftereffect of the simple act of drawing a line?' (Frampton, 2017). Hannah Arendt, in her 1958 book *The Human Condition*, proposed that the public realm in its simplest form was the coming together of people in 'the manner of speech and action' and that wherever people 'gather together … civilisations can rise and fall' (Arendt, 2019). The actual design and layout of the place is not then so important; what matters is that there is a kind of space where people can come together to share 'words and deeds'.

The agora was not a place of complete freedom; however, it was governed by rules and expectations. The freedom to speak and to debate came with a requirement that certain standards of behaviour be kept. And, despite these standards, the agora often became a place of quarrels rather than discussion (Finley, 2002); words were used in civil debate, but they were also weapons to harangue and humiliate, and beyond that disagreements would descend into brawls and even killings (Frampton, 2017). But this too had its value: it was a designated space for a 'controlled explosion', a 'triangle of violence'. This brings us to the idea of the public space as a stage for performance. In the fifth century BCE, the Athenian general and politician Cleon described the Athenians as 'spectators of speeches' (McGlew, 1996), while Plato coined the word *theatrokratia*, 'theatrocracy' of politics as spectator sport (Meineck, 2017). The spectacle of public speech and the role of civility in public debate – especially within the political realm – has been explored in-depth in the previous chapter by Kenny.

The Forum Romanum was similar to the agora, but also different. Nicholas Purcell outlines that open spaces like the forum were much more than just 'voids between buildings' (Purcell, 1989). The forum was a site for transactions of social power, where behaviour, speech and society could be asserted, debated and challenged. The Forum Romanum, in particular, was much more than just a public space; it began as a marketplace and a site for temples, but it also included sites for public speeches and meetings of councils, and for spectacle (Purcell, 2007). Amanda Claridge (1998) writes that it was a 'general purpose open public space for political assemblies (and riots and rallies), committee meetings, lawsuits, public funerals … and public feasts'. Our understanding of both the Agora of Athens and the Forum Romanum as sites for free speech and the practice (or indeed performance) of democracy are coloured by stories and mythologies. The idea that there is a place where debate can occur and a range of opinions may be heard is seen as fundamental to democracy. With the revival of ancient texts and philosophies in the Renaissance in Europe, these ideas became central to the rise of the republican city states in early modern Europe.

The rise and fall of republican civic space in Florence

The performance of power (both real and ideal) was central to the practice of politics in early modern Europe. The public spaces in cities belonged to the public but they were also sites for the performance of political power where rulers could strike a balance between visibility and control. This period is generally characterised as one that saw the rise of absolutism, as in France, and, in turn, saw challenges to this type of rule, such as in the English Civil War. The popes at the head of the papal states maintained a difficult balance between being head of the church and secular rulers. At the same time there were shifts across Europe as many small republican city states formed in the early Renaissance gradually came under the rule of ducal or princely families. Performances of different kinds were used to demonstrate both the power of rulers and of the people, to create mythologies and to enact social hierarchies.

The city of Florence is an ideal example. The Palazzo della Signoria in the centre of Florence was the most important civic space, a place for the populace to vote, to observe their rulers and for rulers to perform their power. The first popular government of the small city republic in the thirteenth century passed laws to control the height of towers on private buildings, a law designed to curtail the domination of public space by various family clans (Atkinson, 2013). The chronicler Giovanni Cavalcanti wrote in the early decades of the fifteenth century that 'whoever holds the piazza [della Signoria], always is master of the city' (Rubinstein, 1995), a statement that should be read not as a declaration of the need for physical control, but of the importance of symbolic and intellectual control of the main civic space and the populace who gathered there. Florence and its civic spaces make an interesting case study for several reasons. The classical origins evoked by the Renaissance humanists demonstrate the importance of historic examples of the role of civic space and the belief that these spaces themselves had a role to play in creating the conditions for a government of the *popolo* (people). The use and events that unfolded in the space demonstrate how civic spaces are subject to control, loss of control and instability, and, finally, the way that civic, or, as we may think of them, 'democratic', spaces can ultimately be subject to manipulation by an oligarchy, and become stages for the performance of civics and liberty that no longer exist in reality.

During the fourteenth century, Florence's central civic square, the Piazza della Signoria, was redesigned into what Marvin Trachtenberg has described as a 'spatiovisual production of power' (Trachtenberg, 1997). This space stood for the civic values of republican Florence, in contrast to the nearby Piazza del Duomo, a symbol of religious power (MacKenney, 2004) and in contrast to the preceding period when powerful families had carved out enclaves within the city and controlled these with force and the construction of towers and other fortifications. The piazza was a symbolic space, framing the seat of republican government in the Palazzo Vecchio, but it was also a real space where militias could assemble, or public events could be held to demonstrate the authority of the government (Trachtenberg, 1997). Spaces like this belonged to the public and their design as open spaces with many streets that fed into it meant that they could as easily become places where crowds could gather and become mobs, or stage an assault on the palazzo itself. This is exactly what happened during the Ciompi revolt in 1378 when woolworkers, who were excluded from guild membership and therefore from positions in the Florentine Government, staged an assault on the piazza and seized the palazzo in an attempt (which ultimately failed) to extend Florentine *libertas* (essentially the freedom from authoritarian or oligarchical rule) from the elites to the workers (Brucker, 1997).

The piazza was used as a gathering place for citizens to participate in plebiscites and to attend the regular inductions of new governments. These 'social spaces' in the early modern republican city state were 'central to the formation, expression and modification of individual and group identities' (Trexler, 1991). Public ceremonies and festivals were transformed into civic ceremonies and these performances of citizenship played a role in integrating rival groups (Brown, 2000). There was, in a sense, no distinction between the performance of politics and its reality. Alison Brown has outlined how the word *rappresentazione* (performance) in Italian had, at the time, as it does now, a double meaning as both a performance of a play and the term for an abstract, symbolic representation of a concept, like 'liberty' (Brown, 2000). So performances were literally conceived of as symbolic depictions of the political system of Florence. The idea of role-playing fitted with the particular system of government in Florence, where office holders were changed every two months, so in a sense the private citizens consciously took on the role of lawmaker and member of government, then exited the stage of government two months later and returned to being a private citizen. When Florence shifted from being a republic to a dukedom and then a principality, citizens criticised the decision-making of the governing bodies as being 'irrational' because it was not reached by open, public debate.

The idea that the piazza was the place of communication and engagement between the citizens and the government is illustrated by a statement from the historian Francesco Guicciardini that when the republic started to fail in the early sixteenth century there was a 'dense fog, or thick wall, between the government palace and the piazza outside', and that the populace therefore lacked any knowledge about how they were being ruled (Brown, 2000). As the city transitioned from a republic to an oligarchy, one of its richest families, the Medici, carefully manipulated existing systems of government and the favour of different powerful rulers. This oligarchy gradually became cemented, first as a dukedom and then a principality. Performance in public spaces was crucial to this transition; it provided a means to create a myth of their right to rule and to present the family as imbued with the qualities of fair and just rulers. The civic spaces that had been symbols of republican Florence and its *libertas* became instead stages for symbolic demonstrations of princely power, new social structures and hierarchies.

In 1589 Florentines were brought onto the streets to celebrate the wedding of the new Duke Ferdinando de'Medici I to Christine of Lorraine. This wedding, one of the most expensive of the Italian Renaissance, represented an alliance between the Medici family and the Duchy of Loraine, part of a program of aligning the Medici with powerful hereditary ruling families across Europe and to further move the city away from its republican history (Blumenthal, 1980). For the arrival of the bride in Florence, the urban and architectural fabric of the city itself was changed through the use of temporary structures and sets. The Via del Proconsolo, which led the wedding party from the cathedral to the old centre of republican government at the Palazzo Vecchio, was adorned with statues of kings of Spain and scenes of great victories of the Spanish over their enemies. This was intended to symbolise Florence's allegiance to Spain, and to present the Medici Grand Dukes as on par with the emperors and kings of Europe's ruling families. As they arrived in the Piazza della Signoria, now renamed the Piazza del Gran Duca, crowds called out Ferdinando's name and he was crowned in front of the Palazzo Vecchio, the old seat of republican government (Gualterotti, 1589). Acts like this allowed the Medici to perform the role of hereditary rulers. They recast the former civic space as a stage for the performance of their princely power and the people of Florence as subjects instead of citizens. Such performances also had an afterlife: they were carefully documented in text and engravings, and records of the more famous events would find their way into the hands of people across Europe. Over the following centuries these performances also gradually shifted from public to private spaces. While some events continued to be held in the streets and piazzas of the city, new spaces, such as large-scale princely gardens and courtyards attached to palaces, were created to host large-scale performances in private or semi-private spaces where rulers had more control over who was present (Wright, 1996). There was a constant tension between control and visible presence. This shift in the use of public space in Florence demonstrates how spaces created to promote free speech, liberty, equality and just rule by the people could be exploited for gaining power and performing a very different type of political power.

The modern city

Over the past century or so the ideal of civic space as a necessary ingredient in the development and maintenance of a democratic society has been at the forefront of many discussions of city design and urban planning. The design of cities and the practice of democracy are frequently linked and the urban space described as a laboratory or an experimental space (Keane, 2013). New designs or redesigns of cities are regarded as having power to shape the future of democracy, implying that they will change the behaviour of citizens. The role of open spaces or civic spaces where citizens come together is often central to these discussions. In 2013, then-Australian Senator Scott Ludlam said that public spaces and 'public experience of face-to-face mixing and mingling of people reminds them of their diversity and commonality, as equals' (Keane, 2013). And cities where this mingling is inhibited by design (whether deliberate or not) are criticised. In Minneapolis, covered walkways above the ground, designed to facilitate ease of movement during cold winters, have separated middle-class office workers from street-level 'have-nots' (Parkinson, 2012), creating inequality and a divided community.

The ideal of a public square and an open civic space in front of, and around, parliament buildings has become central to the design of a modern democratic city. Despite ongoing recognition of the importance of public space in cities, there is debate over whether these spaces are truly a function of democratic government in the twentieth and twenty-first centuries, or just symbolic. In Canberra, a city designed from the ground up as a capital city and imbued with ideals of modern democracy, the National Capital Authority boasts that, 'as the seat of Australia's robust democracy, Canberra provides the Australian community with public spaces for vibrant exchange between the citizenry and their parliamentary representatives' (NCA, 2021). Yet, as John Parkinson, a researcher in public policy has observed, the symbolic openness of Canberra does not actually encourage mingling and engagement between citizens and representatives. On the one hand, the sheer size of the vast open spaces designed to create attractive vistas across the city and surrounding landscape discourages human-scale activity, such as walking, congregating, and incidental or deliberate assemblies. On the other, since 11 September, security and control has limited openness; the Australian Parliament building, which was designed to be easily accessed and walked over, is now restricted by security fencing (Parkinson, 2012). Civic spaces now can be vibrant community spaces, but they can also be tightly controlled and restricted. They might be open for symbolic and approved community engagement such as festivals, but difficult to access for reasons of protest (Hatuka, 2016).

In 2011 in Egypt the retaking of the physical public space of Tahrir Square was arguably as important as the virtual manifestation of protest. Mohamed Elshahed has argued that not only was the physical protest important, but also it symbolised that a public square was a key part of democratic government (Elshahed, 2011). The Mubarak government had recognised the power of public space and deliberately changed the design of the square to inhibit mass gatherings, so the retaking of it was necessary. The real and the virtual public spaces both played a role in the revolutions of 2011.

Twitter as public space

If we decide, then, to accept that Twitter is the virtual version of a public space – if it is our modern equivalent of the town square or the speakers' corner or the agora – we should not forget the inherent inequalities and manipulations of those very spaces. We need to remember that these spaces, while real, also have a mythic, idealised existence. The agora, for example, was essentially off limits to women, at least as a space of speech and influence. We could regard this exclusion as the result of a different time; after all, our modern democracies are more open to diverse genders. However, it can also be a prompt to ask: Who is excluded from spaces of debate now, and how? When historians look back at Twitter, will they observe that it was a place of free speech and democratic debate? Or will they note that it was easily manipulated by those hungry for power with the skills and resources to stage performances and game the system? Will they see the sexual harassment and trolling of women as evidence that, although women were allowed to join Twitter, their voices were not considered equal? What will they make of the manipulation that was allowed to flourish in the name of data collection and the sale of ads: that the importance of commerce trumped democracy?

The performative aspect is also important; visibility in public space is not just about those gathered to watch you, but the afterlife of the performance. In Medici Florence, the appropriation of the public space and its reconfiguration as a stage for the performance of princely power was not just observed by those present. Performances were dutifully recorded by court diarists and engravers, and commemorative booklets were created that were distributed across the courts of Europe. Diplomats present wrote letters describing the events. Likewise, Twitter has become a stage with a much larger audience than just those watching tweets flow past in real time. Various studies have demonstrated that Twitter users are not representative of broader society. A 2019 Pew Research Center study found that Twitter users in the US were:

> Younger, more likely to identify as Democrats, more highly educated and have higher incomes than US adults overall. Twitter users also differ from the broader population on some key social issues. (Wojcik and Hughes, 2019)

However, the audience for Twitter is much larger than just those registered and active as users. In 2012 Donald Trump described Twitter as like 'owning your own newspaper without the losses' (Trump, 2012). Twitter, especially since leaders like Trump have taken to it as a platform of direct and unmediated communication, gets reported on more broadly in newspapers, radio and television. Just like the public square, it is a performance of politics, status and ideology. Just as the Medici shared their conspicuous consumption, the performance of right to rule, it does not matter that everyone is not on Twitter because the audience for the performance is much bigger.

On one level, Twitter is a bit of a mess as a public space: part newspaper, part public square, part commercial platform, part political stage, part virtual water cooler. However, this chaos also perhaps makes it a true civic space. The historian Jacob Burckhardt argued that the word for the activity that described that act of being in the agora, *agorazein*, was intended to convey a mixture of commerce and proximity to temples and offices that was 'mingled with delightful loafing and standing around together' (Burckhardt, 2013). So perhaps online sites like Twitter are indeed civic spaces, just ones that are more real and therefore more messy than our mythic ideal of the historical agora or town square. In the wake of the Christchurch attack in which social media figured so prominently, we might also ponder whether digital space is also more dangerous. The difficulty of control by a central power that Grossman identified in 2009 as a positive when a populace stood up to institutional authority in Iran, has a flipside, where it can be used as a global stage for violent acts against the vulnerable.

References

Aday, S., Farrell, H., Lynch, M., Sides, J. & Zuckerman, E. (2010). *Blogs and Bullets: New Media in Contentious Politics*. Washington DC: United States Institute of Peace. Retrieved from www.usip.org/publications/2010/09/blogs-and-bullets-new-media-contentious-politics.

Arendt, Hannah. (2019). *The Human Condition*. Second Edition. Chicago: University of Chicago Press.

Atkinson, N. (2013). The republic of sound: Listening to Florence at the threshold of the Renaissance. *I Tatti Studies in the Italian Renaissance*, 16(1/2), 57–84. doi.org/10.1086/673411.

BBC. (2011, 9 February). Profile: Egypt's Wael Ghonim. *BBC News*. Retrieved from www.bbc.com/news/world-middle-east-12400529.

Bejan, T. M. (2017, 2 December). The two clashing meanings of 'free speech'. *Atlantic*. Retrieved from www.theatlantic.com/politics/archive/2017/12/two-concepts-of-freedom-of-speech/546791/.

Blumenthal, A. (1980). *Theatre Art of the Medici*. Hanover, NH: University Press of New England.

Brown, A. (2000). De-masking Renaissance republicanism. In J. Hankins (Ed.), *Renaissance Civic Humanism* (pp. 179–99). Cambridge; New York: Cambridge University Press. doi.org/10.1017/CBO9780511558474.

Brucker, G. A. (1997). The Ciompi Revolution. In N. Rubinstein (Ed.), *The Government of Florence under the Medici* (pp. 314–56). London: Faber & Faber.

Burckhardt, J. (2013). *History of Greek Culture*. Courier Corporation.

Cadwalladr, C. (2017, 7 May). The great British Brexit robbery: How our democracy was hijacked. *Guardian*. Retrieved from www.theguardian.com/technology/2017/may/07/the-great-british-brexit-robbery-hijacked-democracy.

Campbell, H. A. & Hawk, D. (2012). Al Jazeera's framing of social media during the Arab Spring. *CyberOrient*, 6(2), 34–51. doi.org/10.1002/j.cyo2.20120601.0003.

Claridge, A. (1998). *Rome. An Oxford Archaeological Guide*. Oxford: Oxford University Press.

El-Nawawy, M. & Khamis, S. (2012). Political activism 2.0: Comparing the role of social media in Egypt's 'Facebook revolution' and Iran's 'Twitter uprising'. *CyberOrient*, 6(1), 8–33. doi.org/10.1002/j.cyo2.20120601.0002.

Elshahed, M. (2011). Tahrir Square: Social media, public space. *Places Journal*. doi.org/10.22269/110227.

Finley, M. I. (2002). *The World of Odysseus*. New York: New York Review Books.

Frampton, S. (2017). Democracy is a clash not a consensus: Why we need the agora. *Aeon*. Retrieved from aeon.co/essays/democracy-is-a-clash-not-a-consensus-why-we-need-the-agora.

Geeng, C., Yee, S. & Roesner, F. (2020). Fake news on Facebook and Twitter: Investigating how people (don't) investigate. *Proceedings of the 2020 CHI Conference on Human Factors in Computing Systems*, 1–14. doi.org/10.1145/3313831.3376784.

Grossman, L. (2009, 17 June). Iran protests: Twitter, the medium of the movement. *Time*. Retrieved from content.time.com/time/world/article/0,8599,1905125,00.html.

Gualterotti, R. (1589). *Descrizione del regale apparato per le nozze della Madama Cristina di Lorenzo moglie Del Don Ferdinando Medici III. Granduca di Toscana*. Antonio Padovani. Retrieved from archive.org/details/descrizionedelre00gual.

Hamilton, J. (2021, 1 March). Social media: Publishers, platforms or something else? *Politics.Co.Uk*. Retrieved from www.politics.co.uk/comment/2021/03/01/social-media-publishers-platforms-or-something-else/.

Hatuka, T. (2016). Public space. In K. Fahlenbrach, M. Klimke & J. Scharloth (Eds), *Protest Cultures* (1st ed., pp. 284–93). New York: Berghahn Books.

Irwin-Rogers, K. & Pinkney C. (2017) Social media as a catalyst and trigger for youth violence. *Catch22*. Retrieved from www.catch-22.org.uk/social-media-as-a-catalyst-and-trigger-for-youth-violence/.

Kavanaugh, A., Perez-Quinones, M. A., Tedesco, J. C. & Sanders, W. (2010). Toward a virtual town square in the era of web 2.0. In J. Hunsinger, L. Klastrup & M. Allen (Eds), *International Handbook of Internet Research* (pp. 279–94). Dordrecht: Springer Netherlands. doi.org/10.1007/978-1-4020-9789-8_17.

Keane, J. (2013, 19 August). Cities in the future of democracy. *Conversation*. Retrieved from theconversation.com/cities-in-the-future-of-democracy-16688.

Liddell, H. G. & Scott, R. (1940). *A Greek–English Lexicon*. Clarendon Press. Retrieved from www.perseus.tufts.edu/hopper/text?doc=Perseus:text:1999. 04.0057:entry=a)gora/.

Low, M. (2009). Cities as spaces of democracy: Complexity, scale, and governance. In R. Geenens & R. Tinnevelt (Eds), *Does Truth Matter? Democracy and Public Space* (pp. 115–32). Dordrecht: Springer Netherlands. doi.org/10.1007/978-1-4020-8849-0_9.

MacKenney, R. (2004). *Renaissances: The Cultures of Italy, 1300–1600*. London: Macmillan Education UK.

Mascaro, C. & Goggins, S. P. (2012). *Twitter as Virtual Town Square: Citizen Engagement During a Nationally Televised Republican Primary Debate* (SSRN Scholarly Paper ID 2108682). Social Science Research Network. Retrieved from papers.ssrn.com/abstract=2108682.

Massanari, A. (2017). #Gamergate and the fappening: How Reddit's algorithm, governance, and culture support toxic technocultures. *New Media & Society*, 19(3), 329–46. doi.org/10.1177/1461444815608807.

McGlew, J. (1996). 'Everybody wants to make a speech': Cleon and Aristophanes on politics and fantasy. *Arethusa*, 29(3), 339–61. doi.org/10.1353/are.1996.0022.

Meineck, P. (2017). *Theatrocracy: Greek Drama, Cognition, and the Imperative for Theatre*. London: Routledge. doi.org/10.4324/9781315466576.

Morozov, E. (2009). Iran: Downside to the 'Twitter revolution'. *Dissent*, 56, 10–14. doi.org/10.1353/dss.0.0092.

National Capital Authority. (2021). *Part One – The National Significance of Canberra and the Territory*. Retrieved from www.nca.gov.au/planning/plans-policies-and-guidelines/national-capital-plan/consolidated-national-capital-plan/part-one#.

Parkinson, J. (2012). *Democracy and Public Space: The Physical Sites of Democratic Performance*. Oxford: Oxford University Press.

Purcell, N. (1989). Rediscovering the Roman Forum. *Journal of Roman Archaeology*, *2*, 156–66. doi.org/10.1017/S1047759400010424.

Purcell, N. (2007). Urban spaces and central places: The Roman world. In S. Alcock & R. Osborne (Eds), *Classical Archaeology* (pp. 182–202). New Jersey: Blackwell.

Rotroff, S. I. & Lamberton, R. (2006). *Women in the Athenian Agora*. Princeton, NJ: ASCSA.

Rubinstein, N. (1995). *The Palazzo Vecchio, 1298–1532: Government, Architecture, and Imagery in the Civic Palace of the Florentine Republic*. Oxford: Oxford University Press.

Saxonhouse, A. W. (2005). *Free Speech and Democracy in Ancient Athens*. Cambridge: Cambridge University Press. doi.org/10.1017/CBO9780511616068.

Trachtenberg, M. (1997). *Dominion of the Eye: Urbanism, Art, and Power in Early Modern Florence*. Cambridge: Cambridge University Press.

Trexler, R. C. (1991). *Public Life in Renaissance Florence*. Ithaca, NY: Cornell University Press.

Trump, Donald J. (2012, 10 November). @realDonaldTrump. Twitter.com. I love Twitter … it's like owning your own newspaper – without the losses. Twitter. Retrieved from twitter.com/realDonaldTrump/status/267286284182 118400 [Archived at didtrumptweetit.com/267286284182118400-2/] (site discontinued). See reporting on tweet in Solon, Olivia. (2017, 5 January). Can Donald Trump save Twitter? *Guardian*. Retrieved from www.theguardian.com/technology/2017/jan/05/can-donald-trump-save-twitter

Urbinati, N. (2002). *Mill on Democracy: From the Athenian Polis to Representative Government*. Chicago: University of Chicago Press.

West, D. M. (2009). The two faces of Twitter: Revolution in a digital age for Iran. *Brookings*. www.brookings.edu/opinions/the-two-faces-of-twitter-revolution-in-a-digital-age-for-iran/.

Wojcik, S. & Hughes, A. (2019). *Sizing Up Twitter Users*. Pew Research Centre. Retrieved from www.pewresearch.org/internet/2019/04/24/sizing-up-twitter-users/.

Wright, D. R. E. (1996). Some Medici gardens of the Florentine Renaissance: An essay in post-aesthetic interpretation. In J. D. Hunt (Ed.), *The Italian Garden: Art, Design and Culture* (pp. 34–59). Cambridge: Cambridge University Press.

9

Crisis, what crisis?

Terhi Nurmikko-Fuller and Paul Pickering

For you know, dear, – I may, without vanity, hint –
Though an angel should write, still 'tis *devils* must print.

Thomas Moore, *The Fudges in England*, 1835.

[W]e live in a time when political passions run high, channels for
free expression are dwindling, and organized lying exists on a scale
never before known.

George Orwell, *New Statesman,* January 1943.

What should ye do then? Should ye suppress all this flowery crop
of knowledge and new light sprung up and yet springing daily
in this city? Should ye set an oligarchy of twenty engrossers over
it, to bring a famine upon our minds again, when we shall know
nothing but what is measured to us by their bushel? Believe it,
Lords and Commons, they who counsel ye to such a suppressing
do as good as bid ye suppress yourselves.

John Milton, *Areopagitica: A Speech of Mr. John Milton for the Liberty
of Unlicenc'd Printing, to the Parliament of England*, November 1644.

I am a big believer in technology and I'm a big believer in openness
when it come to the flow of information … I think that the more
freely information flows, the stronger the society comes, because
then citizens of countries around the world can hold their own
governments accountable … So I'm a big supporter of not restricting
Internet use, Internet access, other technologies like Twitter.

President Barack Obama (O'Brien, 2009)

Our title draws on a well-known headline published in 1979[1] in a tabloid newspaper, the London *Sun*, but it is used here to frame an internal debate. The danger of polemical writing – described in London's *Evening Mail* in 1840 as 'so many words and so few facts' – are well known (*Evening Mail*, 1840, p. 4). Nevertheless, what we offer is a conversation based on opposing assessments of the intersection of communications technologies, history and the current political landscape. The need for such a debate was brought into sharp relief in the aftermath of the massacre in March 2019 of 51 citizens at two mosques in Christchurch, Aotearoa New Zealand. In some respects, the event and their deadly consequences were quickly subsumed into a discussion of the role of social media in providing a platform for a grotesque live feed of the atrocity preceded by the posting of an inchoate manifesto by the perpetrator. What has been largely absent from subsequent debate is consideration of a foundational question: does the broadcast of newsworthy events – no matter how heinous – by various forms of computer technology represent a *profound caesura* in the repertoire of 'political' communication over the long durée?

Put differently, do finely honed algorithms that harvest personal data represent an example of a new departure in political intervention? Does the promulgation of 'fake news' and conspiracy theories via social media exemplify the emergence of a rhizomatic media regime beyond the control of state actors? And, has the spread of the World Wide Web to nearly 60 per cent of the population on earth fundamentally changed the way we conduct our lives and ipso facto our politics? Or have we heard it all before?

In the discussion of broader implications of the Christchurch massacre, we have chosen to focus on text for our sources. Of course, we might have considered these issues through the lens of visual communication, from the semiotics of cave paintings lost in the mists of time to the grotesque images livestreamed on social media platforms as the tragedy in Christchurch unfolded in 2019 (Rahman, 2021; Coaston 2019). Similarly, we could have considered speech, from the first recordings of political speeches that allowed politicians to be in two places at one time and presidential fireside chats utilising radio, to endless chatter online. In the same vein, our unit of analysis might have been song, from ancient revolutionary anthems to the protest songs of the 1960s (Bowan and Pickering, 2017). Why then have

---

1   It is also the title of a Supertramp album that had been released in 1975.

we opted for text? The answer is that, notwithstanding the kaleidoscope of content, the web is primarily a platform for the communication of text based on natural language utterances. Although the Christchurch gunman was anonymised by the fact that we could not see his face and by the fact that the New Zealand prime minister consciously decided not to speak his name, we know him by his words posted online before a shot was fired. Our chronology spans the proliferation of the radical press in Britain c. 1820–50 to the age of online terrorist manifestos (known as 'sh*tposts') such as that posted by the Christchurch gunman, when opportunities for citizens, media organisations and state actors to have their say seem to be limitless.[2]

The historical context for a consideration of these issues is well known, but, for our purposes, is worthy of brief recapitulation. What has been called the 'information–publication paradigm' (Nurmikko-Fuller, forthcoming 2022) can be divided chronologically by two interconnected indices: technological innovation and the relationship between producer on the one hand and audience on the other. Broadly speaking, they are as follows. A period from roughly the fourth millennium BCE when pre-mechanical technologies emerged, which facilitated written communication between individuals and small coteries of elites. A second unfolded between c. 1450 and c. 1850 when successive innovations and improvements in mechanical technology, from Gutenberg's printing press c. 1450 to the steam-driven printing press in c. 1850, incrementally enabled greater communication between the few and the many. The irascible Thomas Carlyle, one of the most influential social commentators of his day, pondered this transformation in his *Heroes and Hero Worship* in 1840, a time when the so-called 'public sphere' (to invoke Jürgen Habermas's well-worn concept) was both fissiparous and febrile. From a pulpit, Carlyle noted, a preacher:

> With the tongue may, to best advantage, address his fellow-men … It is a right pious work, that of theirs; beautiful to behold! … But now with the art of Writing, with the art of Printing a total change has come over that business. The Writer

---

2   As a consequence, the New Zealand Government introduced substantial amendments to the 'Films, Videos, and Publications Classification (Urgent Interim Classification of Publications and Prevention of Online Harm) Amendment Bill' in 2020 (see www.parliament.nz/en/pb/bills-and-laws/bills-proposed-laws/document/BILL_97940, 2020). At the time of writing, the Bill was at the committee stage of consideration by the New Zealand Parliament.

of the book, is not he a Preacher preaching, not to this parish or that, on this day or that, but to all men in all times and places? (Carlyle, 1840a, p. 304)

A third period was inaugurated by developments in electronic communication in the 1920s and 1930s, by which time there was a wireless radio in two out of every three households in Australia (Brett, 1992, p. 19), connecting a few to most. The final period consists of the years since 1995 when technological innovation, in the First World at least, connects not only the vast majority of all persons to all persons, but also automated machines to machines. The conception of the first mechanical general-purpose computers and computer programs occurred in the late 1830s and early 1840s. In less than a century, these hypothetical ideas were turned into general-purpose electronic computing machines, which could do much of the rudimentary intellectual work previously undertaken by women and men. In his groundbreaking 1950 publication, 'Computing machinery and intelligence', Alan Turing, one of the foremost pioneers of computing, began to anthropomorphise its key concepts, referring to 'memory', 'thinking', 'learning' and 'decision'. He even made an overt call for a search to find a 'programme to simulate the [human] mind' (Turing, 1950). This was the seedbed for the invention, some three decades ago, of HTTP (the HyperText Transfer Protocol), and the birth of the World Wide Web. The web has profoundly changed the way information is stored, accessed, retrieved, disseminated, filtered, published, discussed, analysed and consumed.

Today we are all data producers as well as consumers; we are all publishers, including the nameless Christchurch gunman. Has the world been tilted on its axis? Surely we have crossed a Rubicon that irrevocably divides past and present and thus demands new ways of thinking about how we respond to it: harness it for social good, live with it. Or have we simply witnessed an advance in communication technology like many before it, which invariably provokes hysteria and kneejerk reactions and before long is normalised. Crisis? What crisis?

Areopagitica revisited

Although it remains in print almost 400 years after it was first published in 1644, *Areopagitica*, John Milton's ardent plea to the English Parliament to repeal the Licensing Order of 1643 – *An Ordinance for the Regulating of*

Printing – fell on deaf ears. The order was proclaimed at the height of the English Civil War, and designed to suppress pro-Royalist propaganda as well as a proliferation of books, tracts and pamphlets penned by various groups promoting what were considered to be dangerous, radical ideas of democracy and common ownership. In addition to requiring authors to obtain a licence from government censors in order to publish, the ordinance required all printed materials to be registered with the names of author, printer and publisher. It also provided for the search, seizure and destruction of material regarded as 'offensive' to the government and for the imprisonment of any offending writers, printers and publishers. In a climate of fear – perceived or confected or both – the state (according to its leaders at least) required protection from an unholy trinity of warmongering, socially constructed extremist ideas and communication technology. Sound familiar?

Notwithstanding its brief efflorescence during the English Civil War, the *Respublica literaria* in the capacious sense did not begin to flourish in the Anglophone world until the later eighteenth and early nineteenth centuries. Britain's earliest newspapers had appeared at the beginning of the 1700s but they were principally confined to reportage of gossip and society news for an audience of aristocrats and their supplicants. In response to a growing interest in broader news, early in the eighteenth century successive governments sought to impose controls on political content, production and circulation of newsprints, principally by the imposition of a stamp tax. Nevertheless, over the next 100 years the annual circulation of legal newspapers in compliance with the tax grew steadily, reaching 3,000,000 in 1782 (Harris, 1978). By the third quarter of the eighteenth century then, the newspaper as we would recognise it today had come into being. The *Times*, for example, was first published in 1785. Here too, however, the coverage of politics was confined largely to elite machinations and foreign affairs. At this time, circulation of a genuinely oppositional, that is 'unstamped', press remained relatively low (Harris, 1978).

Much changed in the aftermath of the Napoleonic Wars in 1815 when, for the first time, people outside the political nation (the vast majority of Britons) began to demand access to democratic rights. Concomitant with this burgeoning campaign was a sharp rise in the number of radical newspapers in circulation and the appearance of a flood of pamphlets, chapbooks and screeds as well as cheap editions of books considered by the government to be separately and simultaneously seditious, blasphemous or incendiary. The number of newspapers in England and Wales rose from 76 in 1781 to 267 in 1821 (Asquith, 1978). The response of the beleaguered Tory government is significant for our purposes here. Before the end of the year, the parliament had passed what became known as the Six Acts, which included a provision to increase the speed of the administration of justice by reducing the opportunities for bail and allowing for swifter court processing, and a requirement that the permission of a magistrate be obtained before convening any public meeting of more than 50 people if the purpose of the meeting was to discuss matters of 'church or state'. Notably, legislation included an extension of existing laws to provide for more punitive sentences – up to 14 years' transportation – for the authors of seditious writings. Also passed was the *Newspaper and Stamp Duties Act* (60 Geo. III and 1 Geo. IV c. 9), which extended and increased taxes to include publications that had sought to evade duty by publishing opinion as opposed to news. Publishers also were required to post bonds to ensure good behaviour. The government's particular target was those it deemed to be demagogues and scribblers who penned 'irresponsible' and 'positively evil' texts to incite rebellion among those Carlyle later described the 'Dingy dumb millions, grimed with dust and sweat' (Cookson, 1975; Carlyle, [1840b] 1971, p. 217).

A shudder of panic swept through Britain's political elite when it became clear that their stranglehold on access to knowledge, which for generations had buttressed the status quo, was under threat; a new repertoire of political action could tip the balance between ignorance and understanding in favour of the latter. William Lovett and John Collins, prominent working-class activists, made this point from their prison cell in 1840:

> As long as one part of the community feel it to be in their interest … to prevent or retard the enlightenment of all but themselves, so long will despotism, inequality, and injustice, flourish among the few; and poverty, vice, and crime, be the lot of the many. (Lovett and Collins, 1840, p. 73)

For Carlyle, the political implications of the printing press were profound and portentous of an inexorable descent into violence and anarchy. As he put it in (also in 1840):

> Printing, which comes necessarily out of Writing, I say often, is equivalent to Democracy: invent Writing, Democracy is inevitable. Writing brings Printing; brings universal everyday extempore

Printing, as we see at present. Whoever can speak, speaking now to the whole nation, becomes a power, a branch of government, with inalienable weight in law-making, in all acts of authority. (Carlyle, 1840a, p. 304)

Unsurprisingly, the masthead of the *Poor Man's Guardian*, the most important unstamped radical newspaper of the early 1830s, included an engraving of a printing press with the inscription, 'Knowledge is Power'. As an editorial in a radical newspaper put it 1839:

> The Press, in a moral sense, is the only instrument *we can* NOW *employ* to beat down the strongholds of oppression, and those formidable barriers to the happiness and liberty of the People – *ignorance and prejudice*. (*Western Vindicator*, 2005, original emphasis)

It is clear then that by 1820 widespread access to communication technology had transformed the conduct of demotic politics. Suddenly radical news and opinion seemed to be ubiquitous. As one commentator recalled in relation to the *Northern Star*, the preeminent radical newspaper of the 1840s, 'it was not unusual for huge bundles of them to be loaded on carts and driven through the streets in order to lose no time in satisfying the many customers' (Weerth in Kuczynski and Kuczynski, 1971, p. 144). Nor was reading a newspaper, tract, pamphlet or the latest cheap edition of a philosophical treatise a solitary activity conducted as an interior narrative. Single copies of newspapers passed through many hands, were read aloud on street corners, from platforms and in pubs, meeting rooms and homes. Writing in 1903, W. E. Adams, to take one example, recalled a childhood memory of Sunday mornings in his parents' 'humble kitchen' when, 'regular as clockwork', a copy of the *Northern Star*, 'damp from the press', was read aloud to a gathering of family and friends (Adams, [1903] 1968, p. 164).[3] Thus, as Dorothy Thompson has noted, the campaign for democracy was inextricably linked to a struggle for control of the technologies of cheap printing (Thompson, 1984). The government's attempts to staunch the growing demands for political reform were focused on the technology, production, distribution and sale of printed material. They sought to regulate stringently both the spread and the use of technological innovation, rather than respond to the causes of the unrest. Indeed, the Six Acts touched off what later became known

---

3   Adams went on to refer to it as an 'almost sacred text'.

as the 'War of the Unstamped Press'. A sharp rise in the prosecution of journalists, printers and shopmen saw more than 1,000 men and women imprisoned, sometimes multiple times (Wiener, 1969).

But the social order did not disintegrate. By the mid-1840s, the 'War of the Unstamped' was effectively over. The prosecutions ceased and the stamp tax itself was repealed in 1855. Of course, the struggles for reform and social justice continued but, notably, by the middle of the century, printed materials had become normative as a tool of campaigning, employed enthusiastically across the political spectrum. In 1843, for example, the Anti-Corn Law League – a middle-class reform organisation seeking free trade – distributed an estimated 9,000,000 items of literature (101 tonnes' worth), and in 1910 the Tariff Reform League distributed 57 million leaflets and pamphlets in a single year (Pickering and Tyrrell, 2000, p. 22; Trentmann, 2008, p. 101). Speaking as chair of the British Printers' Pension Corporation in 1864, Charles Dickens lionised the men with hands forever stained by ink:

> The printer is the friend of intelligence, of thought; he is the friend of liberty, of freedom, of law; indeed, the printer is the friend of order; the friend of every man who can read. Of all inventions, of all the discoveries in science and art, of all the great results in the wonderful progress of mechanical energy and skill, the printer is the only product of civilization necessary to the existence of free men. (Dickens in Fielding, 1960, p. 325)

Few would have disagreed. If there are no lessons from history, there are at least parallels worth lingering over. There have been several occasions when commentators have declared that we have reached an apotheosis – a technological fulcrum – and the social fabric is confronted with a threat to life and liberty unlike any other. Surely the obverse it true: the internet is today's printing press.

According to John Milton, the Licensing Order of 1643 was nothing short of a 'reproach' to the 'common people', a lamentable lack of trust in their discernment.

> For if we be so jealous over them as that we dare not trust them with an English pamphlet, what do we but censure them for a giddy, vicious, and ungrounded people, in such a sick and weak estate of faith and discretion as to be able to take nothing down but through the pipe of a licenser? That this is care and love of them we cannot pretend. (Milton, [1644] 1980, p. 197)

Areopagitica was a seminal text in shaping modern ideas of freedom of expression. It is reflected, inter alia, in the First Amendment to the United States Constitution but it has little or no place in public discourse today. Does this matter? Does it matter that legislators in 2021 are just as quick to insult the 'common people' in whose discernment they have no faith as they were in 1643? Surely we've heard it all before.

Plus ça change, plus c'est la même chose?

John Keane devotes the final 150 pages of his magisterial study of democracy to pondering the future of his subject (Keane, 2009; Pickering, 2009). His assessment is cautiously optimistic. The growth of what he calls 'monitory democracy', drawing upon 'communicative abundance', has the potential to reassert the role of the populace, perhaps even to instantiate the sovereignty of the people. If not a panacea, 'monitory democracy' – 'viral politics' – would subject the actions of the political class and state actors to greater scrutiny and transparency and foster a range of community associations and pressure groups. As early as the 1990s the idea that a democratised information landscape would lead to a technological utopia became almost hegemonic. Cyber-utopianists, as they were called, were convinced that communication technologies would be transformative, resistant to both corporate and political power (CrowdSociety, 2015). In 1996 a *Declaration of the Independence of Cyberspace*, stated that 'Netizens' were building a 'global social space' independent of tyranny. In the same year, *Magnet*, a widely circulated journal of the cyber-utopianists, proclaimed that the internet would 'enable average citizens to participate in national discourse, publish a newspaper, distribute an electronic pamphlet to the world … while simultaneously protecting their privacy' (CrowdSociety, 2015).

In hindsight, the boundless optimism of the precocious 'Netizens' seems tragi-comic in a number of respects. Ostensibly, the information–publication paradigm has shifted from 'one-to-many' to 'many-to-many' (and ultimately 'everyone-to-everyone'), but, at present, the agency of the 'many' remains a chimera. Today an estimated 4.8 billion, or 58 per cent of the world's population, are connected to the web.[4] As impressive as this number is, clearly not all citizens can access the means to become

---

4   See www.statista.com.

'netizens'. In fact, globally, there is a significant inequality in access to digital technology. According to the International Telecommunication Union's 2019 Annual Report, 82 per cent of people in Europe were connected to the web compared to just 22 per cent in Africa (International Telecommunications Union, 2019, p. 2). Even within developed countries, access is affected by region and class. In Australia, for example, 88 per cent of households in major cities are connected to the internet compared to 77 per cent in regional areas (Australian Bureau of Statistics, 2018).

What is also clear is that data production, collection and dissemination continue to reflect the power and agency of a privileged few. Absolute monarchs of the *ancien régime* dictated edicts; today, media barons determine the content of the evening news. While the internet has enabled an increase in the number of data *producers* – everyone contributes content online – simultaneously, through convergence, the number of data *collectors* and *owners* has dramatically decreased. For example, Facebook owns Instagram and WhatsApp, which means that three different platforms are all harvesting data for one mega-corporation. A recent study shows that just five publishers account for 80 per cent of aggregated online and offline national newspaper coverage in the United Kingdom (Media Reform Coalition, 2019). In other words, a handful of powerful media conglomerates continue to control the distribution of information across all but a tiny percentage of media and platforms.

The promise of a cyber-utopia – a universalist monitory democracy – has proven too overly sanguine if not naive. To be sure, the scandalous, corrupt, excessive and criminal activities of the political establishment and its agents are regularly captured on iPhones, for example, and shared across of plethora of social media platforms, often before they are broadcast by conventional media outlets. But the promised techno-utopia has proven to have a dystopian underside. On the one hand, the internet provides opportunities for government surveillance far in excess of George Orwell's worst fears outlined in *Nineteen Eighty-Four* (Orwell, [1949] 2008). As early as 1992, Neil Postman posed the obvious rhetorical question: 'But to what extent has computer technology been an advantage to the masses of people?' His answer was perspicuous: 'There can be no disputing', he wrote, 'that the computer has increased the power of large-scale organizations like the armed forces, or airline companies or banks or tax-collecting agencies':

> Their private matters have been made more accessible to powerful institutions. They are more easily tracked and controlled; are subjected to more examinations; are increasingly mystified by the decisions made about them; are often reduced to mere numerical objects. They are inundated by junk mail. (Postman, 1992)

In 2011 Evgeny Morozov took up this point, famously railing against what he called the 'Net Delusion'. Far from a tool to destroy authoritarianism, Morozov argued that the internet had become a weapon that authoritarian regimes were putting to good use. Since that time meteoric advances in computer technology have allowed governments to exponentially increase the vast amounts of data they harvest and simultaneously introduce comprehensive metadata retention systems. This is typically justified by the need to combat terrorism (Kininmonth et al., 2018), and much of this has been done with public support. Indeed, it is important to recognise that irrespective of the justification or the objective, as citizens we are agents in our own surveillance. As one of the present authors has argued, whether users are unconcerned or express – or feign – concern about unfettered violations of their privacy, the reality is that they are unwilling to change their online behaviour to protect it (Nurmikko-Fuller, forthcoming 2022). The most compelling element in this data exchange is convenience; as citizens we sacrifice our privacy on the altar of convenience with relentless enthusiasm. Every social media profile we create, every post we publish, every cookie we accept, every page we cache, as well as every bit and byte of information we insouciantly store in the browser, every automated log of geo-coordinates, provides spatio-temporal information to unseen eyes. Who wants to complete tedious bank account details every time we want to buy something online anyway? So, we let technology do it for us. As Morozov notes, the internet is a gateway to pleasure beyond that ever envisaged by Aldous Huxley in *Brave New World* (Huxley, [1932] 2008). 'The Internet has provided so many cheap and easily available entertainment fixes', he writes, 'it has become considerably harder to get people to care about politics at all' (Morozov, 2011).

Clearly, the role of online technology in our politics has been transformative. The first candidate to successfully engage with social media as part of their campaign was Barrack Obama in 2008, his supporters leading the way in online political activism (Smith, 2009). But, it was the 2016 US Presidential Election that provided us with a case in point writ large. Allegations of unprecedented online Russian interference in the political process, complicit with Donald Trump's campaign, are well known, as is the appointment of former FBI Director Robert Mueller as a special counsel to investigate them. Mueller's inquiry lasted nearly two years and involved over 2,800 subpoenas, approximately 500 search warrants and 500 witness statements (Rossman, 2019). Inter alia, the special counsel concluded that Russian-based trolls had systematically conducted cyberwarfare via mainstream social media with the intention of undermining the US electoral system. As Alex Ward has reported (2018), Facebook, Twitter, Reddit, Tumblr, Pinterest, Medium, YouTube, Vine and Google+ were all used. In large part, Mueller's findings were hardly revelatory. Neil Postman (1992) had already noted that users of the internet 'are easy targets for advertising agencies and political organizations'. It doesn't take much of a leap of the imagination to add foreign powers to Postman's list.

The spotlight on the role of computer technology in politics created by the Mueller investigation highlighted that it was not only Russians at work. In March 2018 Facebook came under intensive scrutiny for the fact that the personal data of an estimated 87 million among its 2 billion users had been insidiously accessed by a third party for the purpose of targeting political advertisements. The organisation that had undertaken the hack was a British-based company, Cambridge Analytica.[5] The furore over the raid on Facebook highlighted its vulnerability and undoubtedly damaged the brand, and Cambridge Analytica went bankrupt. Equally, in a politically charged climate, the attention given to the social media behemoth threw a spotlight on its unfettered right to take down content on the one hand and, conversely, its signal failure to control viral posts containing pernicious political material. The company's response has been to implement improved security protocols to protect data sovereignty and the appointment of an external Advisory Board – or so-called 'Supreme Court' – with the power to review Facebook's decisions to take down material, even those taken by the hitherto omnipotent CEO, Mark Zuckerberg (Granville, 2018; Leskin, 2020). Given that there are hundreds of millions of pieces of content taken down every year that can now be appealed, the judgements of a 20-person panel in dealing with the traffic, especially as any individual decisions are overturned, are not to be treated as precedents for similar posts (Leskin, 2020). Moreover, it

---

5   Allegations that the consultants had undertaken similar data harvesting for the Brexit campaign were later proven to be spurious (Kaminska, 2020).

quickly became clear that a modicum of confession meant that all sins were soon forgiven long before the 'Supreme Court' first met. Indeed, in January 2019, the BBC published data showing that not only had Facebook emerged financially unscathed, but also its profits had actually increased (Lee, 2019).

The 2016 presidential campaign also highlighted that alongside mainstream internet sites was a plethora of small-scale, localised, underground and sometimes ephemeral online outlets – 'echo chambers of hate' – hard at work generating, promoting and distributing 'sh*tposts'. Joan Coaston (2019) has noted that the 'manifesto' has long been the platform of choice for spreading right-wing and white supremacist hate speech, but the internet has exponentially increased its capacity to do so. The fact that the heinous incoherent racist manifesto issued by the Christchurch gunman went viral is a case in point. Such sites are unambiguously reprehensible and there is self-evidently no case to be made that they should be protected by the right to free speech.

But elsewhere on the political spectrum the line is not so easily drawn. Keane's hopes for a 'monitory democracy', like the legions of 'netizens' awaiting a techno-utopia, were based on the assumption that the capacity to monitor would inevitably enhance democracy on the side of the angels. The internet has undoubtedly enhanced democracy but the utopia they envisaged has not eventuated. Not all users are those they would regard as angels. Here, it is worth recalling the first of Melvin Kranzberg's laws: 'Technology is neither nor good nor bad; nor is it neutral' (Kranzberg, 1986, p. 545).

In fact, the American public sphere over the past two decades in particular provides an obvious case to examine the intersection between contemporaneous communication technologies – Twitter in particular – and the reporting of political news and opinion. Why America? The list of the top 20 people in the world in terms of Twitter followers in January 2021 comprised mainly entertainers and sportspeople but there were two US politicians among the top five: Donald Trump (88.7 million followers);[6] and, first on the entire list by a considerable margin, Barack Obama (127.9 million followers). Three US platforms providing news

---

6   By this time Trump's account had been suspended and thus he did not feature in this top 20 list. The last recorded figure – used here – would have placed him fourth on the list behind Obama, Justin Bieber and Katy Perry.

content were also among the top 20: YouTube, CNN Breaking News and Twitter itself. The numbers of people following Trump and Obama are vast by international comparison. If we look at the ratio of followers to the size of the overall voting population, the numbers for political leaders in other countries are derisory. While Obama's ratio is 49.8 per cent, Boris Johnson's ratio is 14 per cent and Narendra Modi's is 7 per cent. Of course, the number of followers does not indicate support and nor are followers exclusively domestic, but the trend is there nonetheless.

Unlike Obama, Trump used Twitter as his principal outlet of choice for policy announcements and political commentary both before and throughout his presidency. His obdurate and often incendiary comments on the results of the 2020 election led, ultimately, to his Twitter account being suspended permanently on the grounds that he had incited violence (Collins and Zadrozny, 2021). In this respect, the abrupt end of Trump's access to his principal social media platform was unsurprising but it also raises broader ethical issues in relation to the rights of those in a pluralist society – the land of the free – who use the awesome power of the internet to promulgate their opinions, irrespective of those opinions. Who decides what is 'fake news' or egregious error or a conspiracy theory or simply wacky? Is it Jack Dorsey, CEO of Twitter?[7] Notwithstanding his arms-length 'Supreme Court', are we happy for Mark Zuckerberg to make decisions about who has access to the staggering power wielded by Facebook and Instagram? Who will decide if Fox News or Breitbart News are to be punished for endorsing Trump's views? German Chancellor Angela Merkel, hardly an enthusiastic supporter of President Trump, is one notable political leader who described the permanent suspension of Trump's Twitter account as 'problematic' (Browne, 2021; Merelli, 2021). Here, she was echoing President Obama's unequivocal statement in support of unfettered access to the internet or how it is used. The minute Trump's Twitter account was suspended we might easily imagine George Orwell reaching for his pen.

So, to return to the questions that underpin our polemic. We agree that the potential of immanent technologies has almost invariably provoked grave fears among the political elites who have, invariably, attempted to regulate access to them or suppress them (or both). These efforts have typically been futile. But, political elites are never so easily marginalised.

---

7   Dorsey has stated that he does not 'celebrate or feel pride' about his decision (Phillips et al., 2021).

On the one hand, it is clear that the internet has massively increased the power of a few to collect, store and manipulate data. The use of insidious algorithms, such as those brought to light by the Cambridge Analytica scandal, demonstrate that the internet has aided and abetted those who seek to undermine democracy.

Further, we agree that even among those who understand the scale of digital oppression, many do not care. Agency has not been violently stolen, nor passively allowed to slip away. For perhaps the first time in history we face a situation where we actively choose, even insist on, repeatedly, relentlessly, acquiring each new means of self-oppression. Access to a keyboard has been the agent of inclusion and liberation but this is for good or ill. The promise of a techno-utopia has proven to be a flawed project by the multiplicity of voices admitted to the forum, some wacky, some evil. Here we suggest, with due humility, a revision of the wording of Kranzberg's first law in relation to the data ecology: technology is never neutral; it is simultaneously good and bad.

One of us advocates the view that the advent of the internet has transformed the relationship between the leaders and the led. While previous advances in communication technology have invariably occurred in lock step with an expansion of the political nation, access to the internet is transformative in a way unlike any before it. The advent of the internet has provided citizens with the tools to communicate with each to an extent beyond John Milton's and William Lovett's wildest dreams. The printing press was a profound caesura in the way that the few communicated with the many, but the internet is more impactful: it is a permanent rupture with the past. Many of those who have been given a voice are now beyond the control of political elites and state actors. One of us disagrees.

Indeed, the argument is that for millennia powerful individuals have had the means to present their views irrespective of any semblance of objective truth, however defined. Think of the untrammelled power of media moguls who became household names in the twentieth century. Are Jack Dorsey and Mark Zuckerberg more powerful than Rupert Murdoch, Ted Turner, David Thompson, Frank Packer and Robert Maxwell, or Conrad Black, Lord Beaverbrook and William Randolph Hearst? No. One of us disagrees.

Moreover, one of us argues that the tools used by the purveyors of information will be overtaken by the next technological revolution just as they have been for millennia. Mark Zuckerberg will be a twenty-first century analogue of Ozymandias, the ancient overlord imagined in 1818 by Percy Bysshe Shelley: 'My name is Zuckerberg, king of kings: Look on my works, ye Mighty, and despair!' But, in time all that will remain of an ancient statue of Zuckerberg in the sand will be 'two vast and trunkless legs of stone', a 'colossal wreck, boundless and bare'. Computers will be found next to his ruined statue. Today's political manifesto circulated via a text is no different from a scrap of printed paper with a seditious message being circulated insidiously in 1820. One of us disagrees.

So, does the splintering news market and the ultimately unfettered politics expressed in hypertext herald the rise of a promised utopia of 'monitory democracy' and a crisis quintessentially different from those that have come before? I believe it does; I don't. Huxley's *Brave New World* of self-oppression by pleasure seems more pervasive than he could have possibly imagined. I don't care; I do. Orwell's *Nineteen Eighty-Four* came and went in 1984. In 2084, will citizens wonder what all the fuss was about? I think they will; I don't.

References

Adams, W. E. ([1903] 1968). *Memoirs of a Social Atom* (Vol. 1). New York: Kelley.

Asquith, I. (1978). The structure, ownership and control of the press, 1780–1855. In G. Boyce, J. Curran & P. Wingate (Eds), *Newspaper History: From the 17th Century to the Present Day* (p. 99). London: Constable.

Australian Bureau of Statistics. (2018, March). *8146.0 – Household Use of Information Technology, Australia, 2016–17*. Retrieved from www.abs.gov.au/statistics/industry/technology-and-innovation/household-use-information-technology/latest-release.

Bowan, K. & Pickering, P. (2017). *Sounds of Liberty: Music, Radicalism and Reform in the Anglophone World, 1790–1914*. Manchester: Manchester University Press.

Brett, J. (1992). *Robert Menzies' Forgotten People*. Sydney: Pan Macmillan.

Browne, R. (2021, 11 January). Germany's Merkel hits out at Twitter over 'problematic' Trump ban. *CNBC*. Retrieved from www.cnbc.com/2021/01/11/germanys-merkel-hits-out-at-twitter-over-problematic-trump-ban.html.

Carlyle, T. ([1840a] 1890). *On Heroes and Hero Worship*. London: Chapman & Hall.

Carlyle, T. ([1840b] 1971). *Chartism*. Harmondsworth: Penguin.

Coaston, J. (2019). New Zealand mosque shooting: The shooter's manifesto shows how white nationalist rhetoric spreads. *Vox*. doi.org/10.1111/vox.12907.

Collins, B. & Zadrozny, B. (2021, 9 January). Twitter permanently suspends President Donald Trump. *Washington Post*.

Cookson, J. E. (1975). *Lord Liverpool's Administration 1815–1822*. Edinburgh: Scottish Academic Press.

CrowdSociety (2015). *Cyber-utopianism*. Retrieved from crowdsociety.org/index.php/Cyber-utopianism.

Evening Mail (London) (1840, 11 September), p. 4.

Fielding, K. J. (Ed.). (1960). *The Speeches of Charles Dickens*. Oxford: Oxford University Press.

Granville, K. (2018, 19 March). Facebook and Cambridge Analytica: What you need to know as fallout widens. *New York Times*. Retrieved from www.nytimes.com/2018/03/19/technology/facebook-cambridge-analytica-explained.html.

Harris, M. (1978). The structure, ownership and control of the press, 1620–1780. In G. Boyce, J. Curran & P. Wingate (Eds), *Newspaper History: From the 17th Century to the Present Day* (p. 90). London: Constable.

Huxley, A. ([1932] 2008). *Brave New World*. London: Vintage.

International Telecommunication Union. (2019). *Report on the Implementation of the Strategic Plan,* Document C19/35-E. Retrieved from www.itu.int/md/S20-CL-C-0035/en.

Kaminska, I. (2020, 21 October). Cambridge Analytica probe finds no evidence it misused data to influence Brexit. *Financial Times*. Retrieved from www.ft.com/content/aa235c45-76fb-46fd-83da-0bdf0946de2d.

Keane, J. (2009). *The Life and Death of Democracy*. London: Simon & Schuster.

Kininmonth, J., Thompson, N., McGill, T. & Bunn, A. (2018). Privacy concerns and acceptance of government surveillance in Australia. In *Australasian Conference on Information Systems 2018*. Sydney: University of Technology Sydney ePress. doi.org/10.5130/acis2018.cn.

Kranzberg, M. (1986). Presidential address: Technology and history: 'Kranzberg's laws'. *Technology and Culture, 27*(3), 544–60. doi.org/10.2307/3105385.

Kuczynski, I. & Kuczynski, P. (Eds) (1971). *A Young Revolutionary In Nineteenth Century England – Selected Writings of Georg Weerth.* Berlin: Seven Seas.

Lee, D. (2019, 30 January). Facebook users continue to grow despite privacy scandals. *BBC News.* Retrieved from www.bbc.com/news/business-47065972.

Leskin, P. (2020, 23 October). Facebook's much-hyped 'Supreme Court' that can overrule even CEO Mark Zuckerberg finally launched, but says it won't judge any content about the election. *Business Insider.* Retrieved from www.businessinsider.com.au/facebook-oversight-board-launches-content-moderation-decisions-after-election-day-2020-10.

Lovett, W. & Collins, J. ([1840] 1969). *Chartism: A New Organisation of the People.* Leicester: Leicester University Press.

Media Reform Coalition. (2019, March). *Who Owns the UK Media?* Goldsmiths Leverhulme Media Research Centre. Retrieved from www.gold.ac.uk/media-research-centre/projects/media-reform-coalition/.

Merelli, A. (2021, 12 January). How to make sense of Angela Merkel's criticism of the Trump Twitter ban. *Quartz.* Retrieved from qz.com/1955726/why-world-leaders-are-worried-about-trumps-twitter-ban/.

Milton, J. ([1644] 1980). *Areopagitica: A Speech of Mr. John Milton for the Liberty of Unlicenc'd Printing, to the Parliament of England,* November 1644. In D. Bush (Ed.), *The Portable Milton.* Harmondsworth: Penguin.

Moore, T. (1835). *The Fudges in England.* London: Longman, Rees, Orme, Brown, Green & Longman.

Morozov, E. (2011). *The Net Delusion: How Not To Liberate the World.* London: Allen Lane.

Nurmikko-Fuller, T. (2022 forthcoming). *Linked Open Data for Digital Humanities.* New York: Routledge.

O'Brien, M. (2009, 16 November). Obama: 'I have never used Twitter'. *The Hill.* Retrieved from thehill.com/blogs/blog-briefing-room/news/67865-obama-i-have-never-used-twitter.

Orwell, G. ([1943] 2004). *The Collected Essays, Journalism and Letters.* Boston: Nonpareil Books.

Orwell, G. ([1949] 2008). *Nineteen Eighty-Four.* London: Penguin.

Phillips, T., Ellis-Petersen, H., Walker, S. & Wong, J. C. (2021, 17 January). Trump social media ban sparks calls for action against other populist leaders. *Guardian*. Retrieved from www.theguardian.com/media/2021/jan/17/trump-social-media-ban-jair-bolsonaro-narendra-modi.

Pickering, P. (2009, 19–20 September). A biography of democracy. *Sydney Morning Herald*.

Pickering, P. & Tyrrell, A. (2000). *The People's Bread*. Leicester: Leicester University Press.

Poole, R. (2019). *The English Uprising: Peterloo*. Oxford: Oxford University Press.

Postman, N. (1992). *Technolopoly: The Surrender of Culture to Technology*. New York: Knopf. Retrieved from rws511.pbworks.com/w/file/fetch/68739355/Postman_thamus.pdf.

Rahman, A. (2021, 21 March). Livestreaming bill introduced after Christchurch attacks could criminalise innocent people. *Guardian*. Retrieved from www.theguardian.com/world/commentisfree/2021/mar/15/livestreaming-bill-introduced-after-christchurch-attacks-could-criminalise-innocent-people.

Rossman, S. (2019, 24 March). Nearly 500 witnesses, 675 days: The Mueller investigation by the numbers. *USA Today*. Retrieved from www.usatoday.com/story/news/politics/2019/03/24/mueller-report-trump-campaign-investigation-numbers/3263353002/.

Shelley, P. B. (1818, 11 January). Ozymandias. *Examiner* (London).

Smith, A. (2009, 15 April). The internet's role in campaign 2008. *Pew Research Centre Internet & Technology*. Retrieved from www.pewresearch.org/internet/2009/04/15/the-internets-role-in-campaign-2008/.

Sun (London) (1979, 11 January), p. 1.

Thompson, D. (1984). *The Chartists*. London: Temple Smith.

Trentmann, F. (2008). *Free Trade Nation*. Oxford: Oxford University Press.

Turing, A. (1950). I.–Computing machinery and intelligence. *Mind*, LIX(236), 433–60.

Ward, A. (2018, 17 December). 4 main takeaways from new reports on Russia's 2016 election interference. *Vox*. Retrieved from www.vox.com/world/2018/12/17/18144523/russia-senate-report-african-american-ira-clinton-instagram.

Western Vindicator. ([1839, 28 September], 2005). In J. Allen & O. Ashton (Eds), *Papers for the People* (p. xi). London: Merlin.

Wiener, J. (1969). *The War of the Unstamped.* Ithaca, NY: Cornell University Press.

www.ingramcontent.com/pod-product-compliance
Lightning Source LLC
Chambersburg PA
CBHW041639050326

40690CB00027B/5278